NEW ENGLAND CEMETERIES

PEACHAM, VT.

NEW ENGLAND CEMETERIES

A Collector's Guide

ANDREW KULL

With photographs by the author

Foreword by Barrows Mussey

The Stephen Greene Press

BRATTLEBORO, VERMONT

This book has been produced in the United States of America: designed by R. L. Dothard Associates, composed by American Book–Stratford Press, and printed and bound by The Colonial Press. It is published by The Stephen Greene Press, Brattleboro, Vermont 05301.

Library of Congress Cataloging in Publication Data
Kull, Andrew, 1947–
  New England cemeteries.
  Includes bibliographical references and indexes.
  1. Cemeteries—New England—Guide-books. 2. New England—Description and travel—1951—Guide-books. I. Title.
F5.K84   917.4′04′4   74–27456
ISBN 0–8289–0246–1
ISBN 0–8289–0245–3 pbk.

75 76 77 78 79 9 8 7 6 5 4 3 2 1

Table of Contents

Preface   vii

Foreword   ix

Introductory Note   xv

CONNECTICUT   1

MAINE   45

MASSACHUSETTS   73

NEW HAMPSHIRE   151

RHODE ISLAND   179

VERMONT   201

Additional Notes   237
    Gravestone Rubbing
    Genealogy
    Finding Cemeteries

Acknowledgments   241

Index of Persons   245

General Index   249

Preface

In selecting cemeteries for inclusion in this guide book, I have tried to choose those which, for one reason or another, can be recommended as worth visiting. People who have never paid much attention to the subject tend to think that one graveyard is much like another. In some parts of the country this is undoubtedly the case. In New England, a longer history has included changing attitudes towards death and its proper commemoration. There are cemeteries to please those who enjoy the grand monuments erected in the euphemistic spirit of the Victorians; there are older burying grounds—more characteristic of New England, because they have no equivalent elsewhere in America—where the old slates reflect a sterner theology and the concentrated artistic expression of people who could utilize, and observe, virtually no other medium of the graphic arts. Some people will prefer Mount Auburn, others Concord or Woburn; some people enjoy finding the grave of Daniel Webster or Nathan Hale, while others collect curious and amusing epitaphs. Any one of these sorts of attractions, or any combination thereof, has been regarded as sufficient qualification for this book.

It goes without saying that some cemeteries are more interesting than others. I have resisted the temptation to award stars to my favorites, in the manner of the *Guide Michelin*, thinking that this would provoke more arguments than it would resolve. But I have tried in the descriptions to suggest that, whereas one cemetery truly *vaut le voyage,* another calls for a roadside stop of ten minutes at the most.

The book lists something over 260 cemeteries in the six New England states. Ideally, this would comprise a definitive list of the 260 best cemeteries in New England, balancing their various attributes against each other. I cannot claim such omniscience—though I would venture to say that the margin of error, measured on some absolute scale, does not exceed ten per cent. What is certain is that this book could claim far less authority, and offer far less information, were it not for the generous assistance of a large number of informants, whose names are listed at the back of the book. Some readers will doubtless know of cemeteries which fully deserve to be included, but which have unfortunately escaped my notice. Any such suggestions for additions or corrections will be gratefully received by the publishers.

Of the many people who aided this project, there are three who offered assistance far beyond what could normally be expected: Dr. Hilda Fife of the Maine Old Cemetery Association, Eliot, Maine; Mr. David Dumas of Providence, Rhode Island; and Mr. Stephen Budrow of Pittsfield, Massachusetts. To them I extend my particular thanks.

West Dover, Vermont
July, 1974   A.K.

Foreword

and Clarion Call to the Reader

By BARROWS MUSSEY

To at least one compulsive Yankee rear-view driver, Andrew Kull's new work is an unmixed blessing.

Every so often a book or a hula hoop or a notion like industrial leasing makes you kick yourself for not thinking of it. But perhaps all the disappointed people who didn't hit on a burying-ground Baedeker were simply too close to their subject. A guide to New England graveyards is indeed obvious once you have, as it were, waked up in the cemetery.

Every Yankee child is or used to be brought up on epitaphs handed down in the family (most no doubt improved in transit, *cf*. Mrs. Malaprop), like the one credited to Burlington, Massachusetts—

> Here lies our infant son
> and now he never hollers.
> He graced our home for 14 days
> and cost us forty dollars.

My mother used to dine out on a Presbyterian infant whose memorial was, *We know he died because he sinned.*

My late friend Edwin Valentine Mitchell reported, "The

descendants of a man at Searsport, Maine, are said to have had so much fun poked at them on account of the following epitaph that they had it effaced:

> Under the sod and under the trees
> Here lies the body of Solomon Pease
> The Pease are not here there's only the pod
> The Pease shelled out and went to God."

Not exactly an epitaph, though it might do for one: a true—and what's more, probable—family story of a neighbor near Boston on his deathbed.

Summoning the undertaker, he asked what a decent but not showy funeral would cost. After a quick mental calculation the undertaker gave him a figure.

He drew his checkbook from under the pillow and wrote out a check. "I am taking the liberty of deducting two per cent for cash."

Or take Edward Everett Hale's irresistible memories of *A New England Boyhood:* "I first remember the figures 1826, thus combined, as I saw them on the cover of Thomas's ["Old Farmer's"] Almanac of 1827. Here Time, with the figures 1827 on his head, was represented as mowing in a churchyard, where a new stone with the figures 1826 was prominent; 1825, 1824, and the others were on stones somewhat overgrown by grass and sunken in the ground. The conceit seemed to me admirable, and the date fixed itself on my memory."

As for his seniors, he recalled, "At the elders' table great talk about genealogy: whether Gib Atkins did or did not leave a particular bit of land to certain successors who now own it; whether the Picos and the Robbs were on good terms after the marriage of one of them to an Everett. I will say, in passing, that, as we grew older, we children had the wit to introduce these subjects for the purpose of seeing the mad rage with which different aged cousins advanced to the attack, as a bull might to a red flag."

In short, New England churchyards have attractions from the cradle to the grave.

+ + +

As John Wanamaker supposedly said about woolen blankets, the part that keeps you warm is the part that hangs down. The author of the present volume knows more than he feels obliged to tell you.

He knows more about New England graveyards because he has seen Père Lachaise in Paris and Highgate Cemetery in London. A man who devotes his whole life to a study has no yardstick with which to measure his subject against other subjects (the common fault of local histories and tourist brochures). Mr. Kull, however, is no hereditary sexton: he can see a churchyard as landscape, as history, as architecture, as (forgive me) art, and as copy. This makes him a more enlightening, though less voluble, guide than the Oldest Inhabitant.

To him lettering, cherubim, and weeping willows say more than "How quaint!" Fitz-Greene Halleck is more than (1790–1867), yet less than Shakespeare.

A further attraction of this book depends mostly on the industry of the inquiring reader.

Horace Walpole coined the word *serendipity* to mean *the faculty of finding valuable things by accident.*

Extravagantly though I admire Walpole, I think I have improved his invention (just as the water-wheel was used in

Tibet solely to actuate prayer-mills). I say it is *the faculty of finding things valuable by accident.*

Mr. Kull, for instance, offers you 260-odd choices among the cemeteries of New England. He then invites you to contribute additions—always the way to get the most out of an author's book and reward him to boot.

But beyond this you can find more in the present listings than the author has to tell.

I happened on the entry for Lebanon, Connecticut. Lebanon, Lebanon . . . never been there. Wait. Wasn't that where . . . ?

Yes: Jonathan Edwards on the Great Awakening *(Narrative of many surprising conversions . . . written in 1736).* "There was also the last spring and summer a wonderful work of God carried on . . . in a part of Lebanon, called the Crank [now Columbia, Connecticut.], where the Rev. Mr. Wheelock, a young gentleman, is lately settled." Young Mr. Wheelock became the respected Eleazar Wheelock, founded an Indian missionary school, and in 1770 moved it overland to Hanover, New Hampshire.

Lebanon: Trumbull Cemetery. "Members of the wealthy Trumbull family," says our cicerone. Not just wealthy. Painter Jonathan (1756–1853) was a Revolutionary aide to Washington, a diplomat, pupil of John Singleton Copley and Benjamin West, panjandrum of American art, and eponym of the Trumbull Gallery in New Haven. "For several years the nicely sanded floors, (for carpets were then unknown in Lebanon), were constantly scrawled with my rude attempts at drawing."

His father Jonathan (one of Mr. Kull's three governors) is believed to be the original "Brother Jonathan" who preceded Uncle Sam as our national stereotype.

All this, if you like, is ornamental shrubbery. Now Mr. Kull provides something that was attractive, yes, to his artist's eye, but is also precious to my roving one: "The double portrait stone, in white marble, of Captain Elijah and Eunice Tisdale (both d. 1795), which combines beautiful, sensitive lettering with stylized, primitive-looking portraits." Maybe they were also lifelike. Though I have no evidence beyond names, dates, and surmise, how do you like this? *Elkanah Tisdale, b. Lebanon, Connecticut, ca. 1771, lived in New York as an "engraver and miniature painter" 1794–8, and in the latter year removed to Hartford and joined the Graphic Company, an association of bank-note engravers.* "The designer of the establishment was . . . a fat, facetious gentleman—a miniature painter by profession, but a man of some literary taste, and admirable humor in anecdote." Perhaps Mr. Kull can find his grave for the next edition; my deponent saith only, *was living in 1834.* He wrote "a political Satire called 'The Gerrymander,' and made designs for it."

Terryville, now. The Eastchurch Cemetery has the Tories. The Old Cemetery shows a fairly run-of-the-mill square column with capital, unimaginatively inscribed, "Eli Terry. Died Feb. 24, 1852. Aged 80 Y'rs." Certainly not worth a detour. But Eli was the creator of the American clock industry, using mass-production methods that may have been hinted to him by an acquaintance, Eli Whitney. Your natural assumption that Terryville was named for him is wrong: it was named for his son Eli Jr. (1799–1841), of whom his father rather too modestly said, "I owe my success in life to his perseverance and help over difficulties which I had not power to surmount."

+ + +

The Cemetery in nearly any old New England town may open some such family album before you. Simply start with an entry in *Kull* and go on through the town history, or John Warner Barber's Connecticut and Massachusetts *Historical Collections,* or the *Dictionary of American Biography.* Disinterment for connoisseurs. Genesis to Revelations.

Introductory Note

Throughout the descriptions of cemeteries, readers will notice frequent references to "eighteenth-century stones," "monuments dating primarily from the nineteenth century," and so on. And it will soon appear that the author tends to regard stones from the eighteenth century and earlier as intrinsically more interesting than the later ones. This is not mere antiquarian whim, and the dating by whole centuries is not as casual as it might seem. The watershed in the development of New England carving styles—and, it may be deduced, in the religious attitudes which informed the artistic expression—came, by coincidence, almost precisely at the beginning of the nineteenth century. This is not to minimize the rich variety of styles, originated by different stonecutters, which characterizes the stones of the seventeenth and eighteenth centuries. But the revolutionary change, quickly apparent to anyone who begins to look at New England graveyards, occurred in a very few years around 1800. Stones cut before 1800 may be portrait stones; they may show skulls and crossbones, skeletons, a winged soul, a body in a casket, idealized cherubim or individualized cherubim; they may be decorated with symbols of mortality, symbols of fertility, vegetable symbols, hearts, flowers, vines, sunbursts, sunflowers, hourglasses or clocks. These elements may appear in brilliant artistry or in hack work: but they can be lumped together as the early New England tradition of stonecutting, characterized by individuality of expression, richness of graphic resources, and delicacy of execution. It was, in short, a tradition of art. All of this vanished with surprising suddenness after 1800. The stereotyped urn-and-willow design is suddenly found all over New England. It was replaced in turn by the ubiquitous marble tablets bearing no pictorial decoration whatever; and these gave way to the modern granite "memorials" which—most people will agree—are the least attractive of all. An urn-and-willow design dated before 1795 is a great rarity, as is any of the old styles executed after 1805. The repeated characterization of gravestones by century is therefore intended as a form of shorthand, to let readers know what sort of stones they may expect to see.

All this being said, it must be pointed out that this guide book is in no sense a systematic or scholarly treatment of New England carving styles. Two such works exist, to which anyone seriously interested in the subject is urgently referred. The pioneering study in the field is *Gravestones of Early New England* by Harriette M. Forbes (Houghton Mifflin, 1927; reprinted, Da Capo Press, 1967). A more recent work, more extensive, with a close examination of the religious background to the styles, is *Graven Images* by Allan I. Ludwig (Wesleyan University Press, 1966). Ludwig's book in particular is superbly illustrated. See also *Memorials for Children of Change* by Dickran and Ann Tashjian (Wesleyan University Press, 1974).

Introductory Note

A system of symbols is employed in the text to indicate the nature of the points of interest for which the various cemeteries are recommended. Thus, a gravestone marks a cemetery containing stones with interesting carving or epitaphs. A funeral urn indicates the presence of famous people in a cemetery, or interesting historical associations. The weeping-willow symbol designates a cemetery which is more than usually picturesque. And an obelisk represents the grand, monumental style in cemeteries: Mt. Auburn and its progeny.

INTERESTING CARVING   FAMOUS PEOPLE   UNUSUALLY PICTURESQUE   GRAND STYLE

Maps

Each state is furnished with a map keyed to the cemeteries in the state that are treated in the text. Circles on the maps mark towns in which cemeteries discussed are located. Numbers in the circles refer to the cemeteries themselves, and correspond to the number assigned (in square brackets) to each cemetery in its text description. [A.K.]

CONNECTICUT

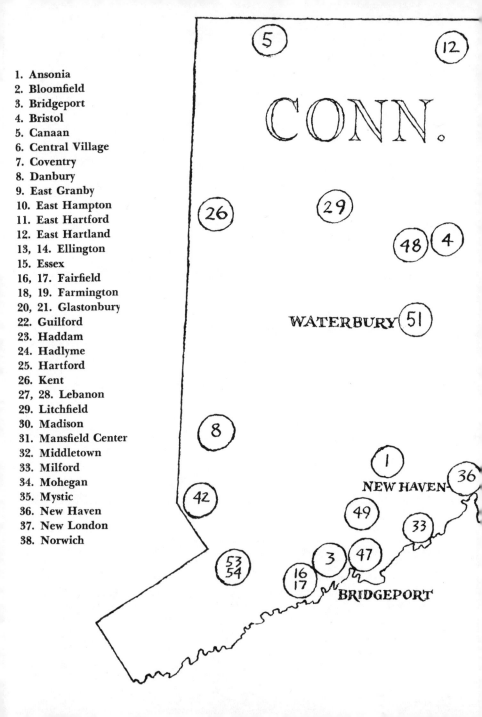

1. Ansonia
2. Bloomfield
3. Bridgeport
4. Bristol
5. Canaan
6. Central Village
7. Coventry
8. Danbury
9. East Granby
10. East Hampton
11. East Hartford
12. East Hartland
13, 14. Ellington
15. Essex
16, 17. Fairfield
18, 19. Farmington
20, 21. Glastonbury
22. Guilford
23. Haddam
24. Hadlyme
25. Hartford
26. Kent
27, 28. Lebanon
29. Litchfield
30. Madison
31. Mansfield Center
32. Middletown
33. Milford
34. Mohegan
35. Mystic
36. New Haven
37. New London
38. Norwich

CONN.

WATERBURY

NEW HAVEN

BRIDGEPORT

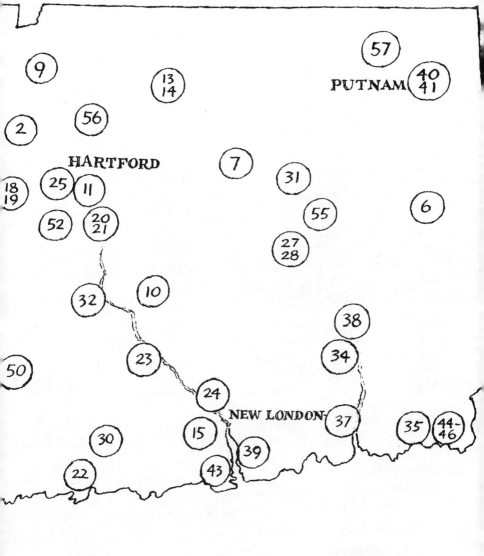

39. Old Lyme
40, 41. Putnam
42. Ridgefield
43. Saybrook Point
44–46. Stonington

47. Stratford
48. Terryville
49. Trumbull
50. Wallingford
51. Waterbury

52. Wethersfield
53, 54. Wilton
55. Windham
56. Windsor
57. Woodstock

FAIRFIELD

*I would rather sleep in the south-
ern corner of a little country
churchyard than in the tombs of
the Capulets.*

EDMUND BURKE

*I have seen beautiful cemeteries.
But it is a form of beauty I do not
care for.*

E. W. HOWE

ANSONIA

Old Town Burying Ground. [1]   On Elm Street, opposite the house identified as David Humphrey's birthplace; just north of the Ansonia/Derby town line.

Several items make this small cemetery worth a brief visit. Among several good eighteenth-century stones is the pleasantly straightforward marker for "The Widow Sarah Tuttle (d. 1769) whose Character in Life was that She was a virtuous woman. . . ." The monument to Lottie N. Chaffee, "beloved and peerless daughter of F. W. & S. A. Chaffee" (d. 1879), is a small example of the Victorian vogue for representations in stone of the broken stumps of trees. The most cheerful epitaph is undoubtedly that of Mrs. Hannah Clark, d. 1801 ae. 91:

> Her lineal descendants at the time of her death, were 333. Viz., 10 Children, 62 Grand Children, 242 Great Grand Children, 19 Great Great Grand Children. During her long life her company was the delight of her numerous friends and acquaintance. . . .

BLOOMFIELD

Old Wintonbury Cemetery. [2]   On Route 189, just north of the village.

A small cemetery with a number of interesting red sandstone markers. The stone of "Hezekiah Goodwin A.M. & Preacher of the Gospel" (d. 1767) bears "His Epitaph compos'd by himself, upon his Death-bed, . . . as follows. . . ." Some distance further back, note the particularly elaborate carving on the stone of Sart. John Hubbert (d. 1760), with a lengthy verse epitaph.

BRIDGEPORT

Mountain Grove Cemetery. [3]   North Avenue (Route 1) at Dewey Street, west of town center.

A large cemetery (140 acres) in the grand manner: the chief interest lies in the more elaborate monuments. The visitor will notice, *inter alia,* a splendid bronze elk on the Jennings tomb; a classical rotunda, a monument to the Warner family; and a Civil War plot marked off by piles of cannon balls. Toward the western part of the cemetery is the grave of Phineas T. Barnum (1810–91), onetime mayor of Bridgeport, a man known to the world for his activities on a wider stage—or under a larger tent. His monument is large and solid but—considering his career—disappointingly subdued. What might be said to have been Barnum's real monument is, regrettably, no more to be seen. This was the memorial erected by Barnum to General Tom Thumb, his famous midget. It stood across the road from the Barnum tomb and consisted originally of a marble shaft forty feet high, topped by a life-size statue of Tom Thumb—in real life Charles S. Stratton, who died in 1883 at the age of forty-five. Sadly, the column cracked and had to be lowered; the statue itself was twice decapitated; on the most recent occasion (in 1974) the head was later discovered in a hollow tree, but the body of the figure had been broken beyond repair.

BRISTOL

 Downs Street Cemetery. [4]   On Downs Street, just south of Riverside/Memorial Boulevard (Route 72), east of the town center.

A small, old graveyard with a semi-abandoned air. It is a pleasant, shady spot, although the noise of traffic is intrusive. Several of the American ancestors of Sir Winston Churchill are buried here. Note particularly, among the handsome markers in red sandstone, the double stone for Deacon Elnathan Ives and his Consort Abigail. The large tomb of the Rev. Samuel Newell (d. 1789) is an example of beautiful lettering.

CANAAN

 Mountain View Cemetery. [5]   West of Route 7 on Sand Road, which leaves Route 7 to the southwest, one mile south of Canaan village.

An extensive cemetery, well kept, still in use; the main interest is in a number of eighteenth-century stones in the section nearest the road. Note on these old slates the extreme simplicity of style: most of them employ an attractively stylized sunburst motif. There are graves of many Revolutionary soldiers, including the broken stone (marked by a flag) of Capt. Gershom Hewitt, "who through a ruse, secured the plans of Fort Ticonderoga for Col. Ethan Allen" before its capture May 10, 1775.

C E N T R A L   V I L L A G E

Evergreen Cemetery. [6]   On Route 12, south of the village.
A very ordinary cemetery except for one touching monument.
By the south wall, about halfway back, is a marble memorial to
Elisha Cady, d. 1880. Whoever designed it chose to record
Mr. Cady's great pleasures in life, with the result that we gain
a more vivid impression of Elisha Cady than of many a leading
citizen whose eloquent epitaph attests at length to his charity,
his piety, his all-round solidity. On one side of the monument
is a relief portrait of a cow. The legend reads:

> Rosa, My first Jersey Cow
> Record 2 lbs. 15 ozs. Butter
> from 18 quts. 1 day milk.

On the other side is engraved a fiddle with its bow, and the
superscription, "All ready, Mr. Cady." (Mr. Cady tucks the
instrument under his chin, lifts his head to give the signal—
and the little group in the parlor strikes up a waltz. . . .)

C O V E N T R Y

Nathan Hale Cemetery. [7]   On a hill overlooking Coventry
Lake; the road to the lake starts north of the village from the
intersection of Routes 31 and 275.

The birthplace of Nathan Hale, the Revolutionary patriot, is
three miles down the road; at the edge of this cemetery is a
large granite obelisk in his memory. Hale was a schoolteacher
who joined the Connecticut Militia and volunteered to undertake dangerous espionage in the vicinity of Long Island. He
was captured by the British and executed without trial in New
York in 1776. He was reported to have said, while standing on

the gallows, "I only regret that I have but one life to lose for my country." Hale was twenty-one years old.

To the northeast of the obelisk is the Hale family plot. Here is a large slate stone placed by Deacon Richard Hale in memory of his two sons, neither of whom could be buried in Coventry. This stone was Nathan Hale's monument long before the massive nineteenth-century obelisk was erected; he shares it with his brother, Richard Hale, Jr., who "died of a consumption in the Island of St. Eustatia," in 1793. There are many more eighteenth-century stones in this attractive cemetery: many follow the classic designs but with only modest technique, giving a "primitive" version of the familiar soul-and-wings motif—none the less interesting for that.

DANBURY

Wooster Cemetery. [8] At the end of Ellsworth Avenue, north of the town center.

A large, nineteenth-century cemetery, for the most part rather ordinary; there are nevertheless a few points of interest. The impressive monument in red sandstone, surmounted by an eagle, marks the grave of Brigadier General David Wooster of the Revolutionary War. General Wooster's career had its ups and downs. In 1776 he was briefly in command of American forces in Quebec, but was recalled by the Continental Congress because of incompetence. In 1777, however, he valiantly led the defense of Danbury against the Tory Raids of William Tryon: and he died of his wounds from this engagement.

Near the Wooster monument the stone of Austin Walbridge (d. 1889) is decorated with a locomotive in relief. Not far off is the handsome Soldiers' and Sailors' Monument, a memorial to Danbury's Civil War veterans.

In a newer part of the cemetery is the grave of Charles Ives (1874–1954), by all odds the most famous man buried here. Ives was a native of Danbury; he is increasingly considered to be America's greatest composer. Much of Ives' music contains reminiscences of popular music (folk songs, band concerts, parades) heard in Danbury as a boy.

EAST GRANBY

Old Burial Ground. [9] On Route 20, across from the savings bank.

A small cemetery, on a knoll behind a white fence. It attracts attention because of its particularly fine collection of handsome, well-preserved stones, offering good examples of eighteenth-century carving in both slate and red sandstone. As a superb example of the latter note the gravestone (centrally positioned) of Mr. John Thrall.

EAST HAMPTON

East Hampton Cemetery. [10] East of the village on Route 66: on a knoll across from Pocotopaug Lake.

The older part of this cemetery is of some interest, though not by any means worth a detour. Among the old stones (primarily brownstone) are several handsome examples: note in particular the large adjacent stones of the Reverend Lemuel Parsons and his "amiable and virtuous consort," Katharine. There is an attractive view from the top of the hill.

EAST HARTFORD

Center Burying Ground. [11]   In the center of town at 946 Main Street (Route 5).

A large, well-kept cemetery. The old section contains a great many eighteenth-century stones in red sandstone, brownstone, and granite.

EAST HARTLAND

Old Burying Ground. [12]   On Route 20 at the village center, next to the village store.

The oak trees along the front of this pretty, well-kept cemetery are said to be descended from Hartford's famous "Charter Oak," the legendary tree in which the colonial constitution of Connecticut was once hidden—according to the story—to keep it from British hands. Within are the graves of eighty-one Revolutionary soldiers. Two monuments near the center consist of old millstones which were used to grind grain for the soldiers mustered from Hartland. Close to these is a "noon stone," a kind of sundial, made up of a vertical stone standing on a horizontal one. When the shadow of the vertical stone comes in line with the mark chiselled beneath it, it should be noon—or thereabouts.

ELLINGTON

Ellington Cemetery. [13] At the center of the village; entrance is via a driveway leading off the green.

For a small town Ellington has a relatively extensive cemetery: its front entrance is by the village green, and at the far back it borders on farmers' fields. It is attractively maintained. The older section, near the entrance, contains a number of interesting eighteenth-century stones. At the far back is a Jewish cemetery, with modern monuments bearing Hebrew inscriptions.

Two graves of particular local interest are marked by small arches. One is the grave of Samuel Phinney, the first settler: an inscription describes how he came to Ellington in 1717. The second arch is set over the original gravestone of Margaret Thompson, who left Scotland with her husband and nine children, intending to emigrate to America. Her husband died in Ireland, and Mrs. Thompson brought the children herself, settling here in 1720.

McKinstry Cemetery. [14] Behind the library at the end of the green.

The visitor to Ellington should pause for a brief visit to this small cemetery. It is unusual in that it remains in private hands, belonging to the last surviving member of the McKinstry family, even though it stands square in the middle of the village. It is kept locked, but most of the stones can be seen fairly well from outside the fence.

The first member of the family to arrive in Ellington was the Rev. John McKinstry, who was passing through the district with his family when his wife became ill. McKinstry was asked to remain and organize a church. The new minister did not always see eye to eye with his parishioners on matters of doctrine, and at his death he declined to be buried in the Ellington Cemetery with everyone else. Thus the McKinstry family cemetery was established on private land. The gravestone of his son, Alexander McKinstry, bears an interesting epitaph which concludes with these lines:

> Neighbor the unhappy
> hous looks Diselate &
> Mourns & Every Door
> Groans doalful as it turns
> The Pillars Languish and Each
> Silent wall in Greaf lament
> The Masters Fall, who Departed
> this life Novr. the 9th, 1759
> in the 30th Year of his Age.

ESSEX

Riverside Cemetery. [15] Off North Main Street: the road into the cemetery leads through a gate, sharply to the east (downhill), just north of the village center.

The setting of Riverside Cemetery, above and along the shore of the Connecticut River, is very fine: a touch of grandeur is added by a double file of carefully trimmed yew trees on either side of the main drive, running the length of the cemetery. The oldest section, close to the river, contains a considerable number of eighteenth-century gravestones (mostly red sandstone). But the most interesting monuments here are the more elaborate ones of the nineteenth century, and two in particular, both well to the back of the cemetery. One of these is a marble monument to two Captains Urquhart, of which the

BRIDGEPORT

west side shows a lighthouse in deep relief; the other, also in marble, is a beautiful monument to William W. Stevens, "lost off Sandy Hook November 20, 1861, aged 23 years." Atop the monument is a lady holding an anchor; the front of the pedestal bears a magnificent sailing ship in relief.

FAIRFIELD

Greenfield Hill Cemetery. [16]   On Bronson Road, in the Greenfield Hill district (northwest of Fairfield village) .

An attractive, well-kept cemetery, located on a gentle slope behind a handsome stone wall. In use since the 1740's, with one "homemade" stone apparently dated 1737. The cemetery contains the graves of ninety-eight Revolutionary soldiers; their names are listed on a plaque by the gate. There are fine examples of carving in slate and red sandstone—note, among others, the generously proportioned stone of Samuel Bradley (d. 1772) , along with his footstone which has been uprooted and is leaning nearby.

Old Burying Ground. [17]   Beach Road, near the town center: south of the village green.

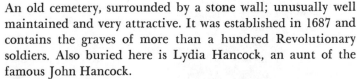

An old cemetery, surrounded by a stone wall; unusually well maintained and very attractive. It was established in 1687 and contains the graves of more than a hundred Revolutionary soldiers. Also buried here is Lydia Hancock, an aunt of the famous John Hancock.

Existing stones in slate and red sandstone go back to the early eighteenth century; some of the red ones are unusually large. A number of the slate stones have evidently been replaced by modern copies. One curious anomaly can be observed not far from the main entrance—namely, two adjacent gravestones for Mrs. Abigail Squier, Wife of Samuel Squier Esq., identical in design and wording except that one stone has her d. 1780 ae. 55, while the other, apparently much more recent, maintains that she d. 1785 ae. 52. Next to these conflicting stones is the unequivocal grave of Samuel Squier Esq. himself, with the epitaph:

> Praises on tombstones are but vainly spent
> Assured life to come is our best Monument.

FARMINGTON

Old Cemetery. [18] On the east side of Main Street (Route 10), south of the village center.

The old cemetery in the pretty town of Farmington contains a large and unusually good collection of old stones, dating from the early eighteenth century. Many are marked by the characteristic, strangely wide-eyed faces found in this area.

As at many of New England's grandest cemeteries, the entrance is through an "Egyptian" gateway. But unlike New Haven's Grove Street, for instance, the gateway here is rather small and made of wood.

Riverside Cemetery. [19] At the end of Maple Street, one block west of Main Street (Route 10), south of the village center.

The entrance to Riverside Cemetery is a short walk from Farmington's Old Cemetery. It is worth a visit to see two items in particular. Riverside Cemetery occupies the site of an old burying ground of the Tunxis Indian tribe: at the end of the central driveway is a brownstone monument commemorating the tribe and some of their famous battles.

Halfway along the central drive is a small marble tablet in memory of Foone, an African who was involved in a famous mutiny aboard a slave ship.

F O O N E

A native African was drowned while bathing in the centre basin August 1841. He was one of the company of slaves under Cinque, on board the Schooner Amistad who asserted their rights & took possession of the vessel after having put the Captain, mate & others to death, sparing their masters Ruez & Montez.

In August of 1839, a mysterious ship was sighted several times off the east coast of the United States. It flew no flag; its sails were in tatters; the men aboard were seen to be black and half dressed, and they spoke no English. Attempts were made to take the strange vessel in tow, but the black men managed to cut loose again. Finally, on August 26, a landing party from the ship surprised the residents of Montauk, Long Island. The Coast Guard arrived on the scene; eventually two white men emerged from the ship, one of whom spoke English.

The ship, he said, was the Spanish schooner *Amistad*. She had set sail from Havana June 28 on a coastal voyage, with a cargo of fifty-three slaves, a quantity of gold doubloons, and various luxury goods. Four days out the slaves had somehow got free of their chains. They had killed the captain and the cook; two other Spanish crewmen had jumped overboard. The two remaining Spaniards, Montes and Ruiz, had been spared after promising to help navigate a passage back to Africa. Pending an investigation, the ship with its cargo was then towed to New London. The mutineers were jailed first in New Haven, then in Hartford, to await trial.

Under such circumstances, the arrival in New England of a party of slaves brought about a tremendous upsurge of abolitionist sentiment. The "Amistads" became great objects of curiosity, and people flocked to the Hartford county jail to have a look at them. The men had been taken together from an area called Mende, in what is now Sierra Leone; they were, therefore, fellow-countrymen. Their acknowledged leader, and the one who quickly achieved the greatest celebrity, was called Joseph Cinque: he was a striking figure, and gave all visitors an impression of courage and brilliance.

An *Amistad* defense committee was formed, composed principally of abolitionists and missionaries, to take the part of the slaves during the complicated legal proceedings which were now underway. The Spanish government claimed the ship and her cargo, and wanted the men deported to Havana to stand trial for mutiny and murder. The attitude of the United States government was, to put it politely, equivocal: the prosecution was directed by the U.S. Attorney for Connecticut, and President Van Buren, sure of the outcome, had directed that a naval vessel stand by in New Haven harbor to deport the men instantly to Havana. But at the first trial, at New Haven in January, 1840, the "Amistads" were declared to be free men, not salvage; it was directed that they be "delivered to President Van Buren for transport back to Africa." The government appealed this decision to the Supreme Court. John Quincy Adams was prevailed upon to undertake the defense, in his last courtroom appearance. Eventually, the Connecticut decision was upheld.

In its decision the Supreme Court did not, however, direct that the ex-slaves be transported back to Africa. They were free men, no longer imprisoned, but they lacked the funds with which to return home. It was during this period, in the summer of 1841, that the men lived in a barn in Farmington. While the money was being raised, they were saturated with religious instruction by their missionary friends, and plans were laid to establish a mission in Sierra Leone on the occasion of their return home. Cinque and some of the others went on a tour of the northeast, performing songs and recitations. The men left behind in Farmington grew despondent, thinking perhaps that they had been abandoned. It was at this point that Foone drowned while swimming in the town pond. He was a young man and a strong swimmer; and the others were convinced that he had committed suicide, in despair of ever getting back to Mende.

The money was raised, in large part by Cinque's touring company, and the men embarked in November, 1841, after farewell celebrations in Farmington and New York. An American mission was duly established at Freetown. Out of the *Amistad* defense committee grew the American Missionary Association, which is still in existence: the Association is best known for its rôle in founding colleges for freed slaves in the American South, including Hampton Institute and Fisk and Howard Universities.

For the full story of this fascinating episode, see *Black Odyssey* by Mary Cable (Viking, 1971).

G L A S T O N B U R Y

 Green Cemetery. [20]   On the town green, near the junction of Main and Hubbard Streets.

The oldest cemetery in Glastonbury: the original graveyard on the green was established in 1692. There are many interesting items among the old stones, a few of which deserve special mention. Near the western end is a small marker in red sandstone for Marcy Halle (d. 1719), with its notable epitaph:

> Here lies one wh
> os lifes thrads
> cut asunder she
> was strucke dead
> by a clap of thundr.

Close to the southern edge of the old section is the slate stone of Deacon David Goodrich,

who on the 7th of June
AD 1779
at his Evening Prayer
Fell Down in an instant
and never saw to make
any Motion after
Being in the 74th Year
of his Age.

Less pointed than these, but worth finding, is the epitaph
of Doctor Elizur Hale (d. 1790). After recounting his long and
useful career it concludes as follows:

At his Death all Classes participated in the deepest
mourning, lamenting the departure of their Physician
and Friend.
The Sage is Gone.
This modest Stone what few vain Marbles can,
May truly say here lies an honest man,
Foe to loud praise, and Friend to learned ease,
Content with Science in the vale of Peace,
Calmly he look'd on either Life, and here
Saw nothing to regret or there to fear;
Let him accept these Rites a Stone a Verse
Tis all his Children, all his Friends can give.

Old Eastbury Burying Ground. [21]   On Manchester Road
(Route 83), ½ mile south of Hebron Avenue (Route 94).

This small cemetery was established in 1733 to serve the community at the far eastern end of Glastonbury. It contains one
famous stone, the brownstone marker at the rear of the yard
for the four sons of Mr. Appleton and Mrs. Lydia Holmes.
One son, Burridge, died in December, 1794; Ozias, Appleton,

and Calvin died on three successive days in February, 1795. The stone bears four stylized, somewhat Egyptianate portraits of the boys, with a representation of the truncated family tree. The epitaph reads (in part) :

> The afflicted mother weeps from day to day
> To see those lovely branches torn away.
> But whilst you weep the Lamb on Calvary slain
> Feeds the young branches which shall sprout again
> Whilst God the FARTHER who all heaven supplies
> Shall wipe the sorrows from the parents eyes.

GUILFORD

Alderbrook Cemetery. [22]   Boston Street, east of the village center.

Orderly and well maintained; a number of eighteenth-century stones, most of them leaning in a row against the wall by the road. These were moved from the village green, which was the original burying ground in Guilford. The cemetery would be of no more than ordinary interest were it not for the grave (marked by a granite obelisk at the head of the central drive) of Fitz-Greene Halleck (1790–1867), "One of the few, the immortal names / That were not born to die."

The poetry of Fitz-Greene Halleck has lain in such obscurity for so many years as virtually to demand an academic "revival." Born in Guilford, he was first known to the public through his lighter works —the humorous "Croaker Papers," written by Halleck together with Joseph Rodman Drake, and a long satire, *Fanny*, in the style of Byron's *Beppo*. Halleck and Drake were numbered among the group known as the Knickerbocker Wits. Among Halleck's serious verses, the two best known poems were "Marco Bozzaris"—the concluding lines of which supply Halleck's epitaph—and the elegy on the death

of his friend Drake. Its opening stanza was a familiar strain at count-
less school recitations:

> Green be the turf above thee,
> Friend of my better days!
> None knew thee but to love thee,
> Nor named thee but to praise.

No less an authority than Rufus Griswold asserted that "Halleck
must be pronounced not only one of the chief ornaments of a new
literature, but one of the great masters in a language classical and
immortal." Halleck served for many years as private secretary to
John Jacob Astor, who was, at the time of his death in 1848, the
richest man in the United States.

HADDAM

Thirty Mile Island Cemetery. [23]   Main Street (Route 9A),
in the center of town, opposite the flagpole.

An exceptionally pretty setting running downhill from the
road, enhanced in the spring by flowering trees and wild-
flowers. The old cemetery (established 1662) is well looked-
after without being vigorously spruced-up: there is a pleasing
air of graceful decay. The oldest legible stones date from the
eighteenth century (mostly red sandstone), and a few are
particularly attractive; still it is the overall ambience that
makes this graveyard such a charming one.

HADLYME

Congregational Churchyard. [24]   On Route 82, north of the
village.

Not sufficiently old or important to merit a detour, nevertheless an attractive stop for those in the vicinity: a charming

setting on a hillside above a small river. The stones are the usual mixture, but with some very striking calligraphy on some of the nineteenth-century marble tablets. There is a large number of Comstocks buried here—cousins, perhaps, to Anthony Comstock, organizer of the New York Society for the Suppression of Vice; he was a Connecticut man but not, unfortunately, from Hadlyme.

HARTFORD

Ancient Burying Ground. [25] Behind Center Church at Main and Gold Streets, just south of Thomas Hooker Square.

In June, 1636, Thomas Hooker brought his congregation with him from Massachusetts to settle in Hartford. It was the first year of the Connecticut River settlements. Center Church in Hartford is the church that Hooker established, and the Ancient Burying Ground was the settlers' graveyard.

Many of the brownstone markers in this historic cemetery are in excellent condition. A few would seem to be in a near-miraculous state of preservation: these are evidently replicas of the originals, and the copies have been beautifully made. Sharpness of detail never lasts as well in red or brown stone as it does in slate, so these replacement stones provide an idea of the results originally achieved by the carvers who worked in red sandstone. One of these stones, very curiously, has the epitaph first, as it were, and the obituary second; the epitaph is inscribed on a piece of marble, set into the brownstone—

> Drowned in the glory of his years
> And left his mate
> to drown herself in tears

> Doctr. Thomas Langrell of Hartford
> Departed this life as above on
> June the 15th A.D. 1757. . . .

There are several impressive table stones for prominent citizens. A verse epitaph for Samuel Stone (d. 1663) concludes:

> Errors corrupt by sinnewous dispute
> He did oppugne, and clearely them confute:
> Above all things, he Christ his Lord prefer'd
> Hartford! thy richest jewel's here interd.

KENT

Flanders Cemetery. [26] On Route 7, two miles north of Kent village.

A small roadside cemetery of more than usual interest: it offers interesting stones dating back to 1760 and a fine view of the Housatonic Valley. Note in particular the double headstone (in red sandstone) of the daughters of Dr. Oliver Fuller (d. 1793) ; also the proliferation of sunflower designs on stones of the early nineteenth century. The real prize here is perhaps the slate stone of Capt. Jirah Swift, d. 1776 ae. 39, with its epitaph:

> I in the Prime of Life must quit the Stage,
> Nor see the End of all the Britains rage:
> Farewell my wife & my eight Children dear,
> God will be gracious, never yield to Fear.

> He was one of those unfortunate soldiers
> that went to the northward & died on his
> return.

LEBANON

Liberty Hill Cemetery. [27] On the east side of Route 87, three miles north of Lebanon village.

An agreeable nineteenth-century cemetery in a peaceful, wooded, hillside setting. The chief interest is the grave, in the center at the far back, of Captain S. L. Gray. Captain Gray was a whaling skipper who died in 1865 when his ship, the *James Murray*, was shelled by the Confederate raider *Shenandoah* off Guam. His body was preserved in a cask of spirits and buried here by his wife, still in cask.

Trumbull Cemetery. [28] On Route 207, ¾ mile east of Lebanon village.

Pleasantly situated on a knoll, in farming country. There are buried here three governors of Connecticut, all members of the wealthy Trumbull family, as well as William Williams, a signer of the Declaration of Independence. Many graves of Revolutionary soldiers, some with good epitaphs: for instance Col. James Clark, d. 1826 ae. 96, "He was a Soldier of the Revolution, and dared to lead where any dared to follow. . . ."

Among many interesting stones note in particular the double portrait stone, in white marble, of Captain Elijah and Eunice Tisdale (both d. 1795), which combines beautiful, sensitive lettering with stylized, primitive-looking portraits.

LITCHFIELD

East Cemetery. [29] East of the village center on Route 118.

Litchfield's East Cemetery was established in the 1750's as the town's second burying place. There remain several interesting stones in the original section. The prize item is the white marble stone of Mr. Richard Wallace (d. 1794), with a grape-vine motif of exceptionally fine detail.

M A D I S O N

West Cemetery. [30]   On Route 1, west of the village.

Does not merit a detour, but worth a stop for those passing by. A fair number of eighteenth-century stones (in red sand-stone), most of them bearing the cartoon-like faces character-istic of the area. There is a fine sailing ship on the marble slab at the grave of Captain Alfred G. Dowd (d. 1853), next to the drive through the center of the old section. Behind Captain Dowd is the broken stone of a Civil War veteran: the remain-ing lower half reads, "After serving his country three years he came home to die." One small, thick red stone—evidently less old than the date it bears—marks the grave of Samuel French, d. 1688 ae. 6; it concludes, "and he was the First Corps Buried here."

M A N S F I E L D   C E N T E R

Old Cemetery. [31]   In the village, on Route 195.

A small, simple roadside cemetery, containing stones of much more than usual interest. There is a large number of old slates, offering an extraordinary variety of eighteenth-century styles: one row of stones, primarily graves of the Conant and Wil-liams families, shows the full range from primitive to highly sophisticated carving. Many fine stones mark graves of the Storrs family (the town of Storrs is just up the road), and a large granite monument, erected in 1879, traces the history of the Storrs family in America. The stone of Mrs. Bridget Snow (d. 1768), by the northern wall, is a good example of the design which represents the body of the deceased in its coffin.

MIDDLETOWN

Riverside Cemetery. [32]   St. John's Square, in the north end of town, overlooking the Connecticut River.

An attractive and historic cemetery which is unfortunately kept locked: the key is available on request at the fire station on Main Street.

The cemetery was established in 1689 on the site of the first meeting house. There is a large number of eighteenth-century graves, marked almost exclusively by red or brown stones. A large monument marks the grave of Commodore Thomas Macdonough (1783–1825), victor of the Battle of Lake Champlain on September 11, 1814. In that "murderous engagement," fought off Plattsburg, N.Y., Macdonough defeated a superior British fleet by consummate tactics and handling; it was to prove the decisive naval battle of the War of 1812.

MILFORD

Milford Cemetery. [33]   Entrance on Prospect Street, north of the railroad tracks, by the D.A.R. headquarters.

Milford Cemetery, which appears at first to consist of an endless expanse of modern granite "memorials," does in fact contain an old section which is extensive and highly rewarding. The older part is at the southern end of the cemetery, near the railroad tracks; it has a mildly decrepit air about it, but contains much that is of interest.

Two colonial governors of Connecticut are buried here, Robert Treat (1622–1710) and Jonathan Law (1674–1750). Treat, in particular, had a distinguished and wide-ranging career: at one point, discontented with affairs in Connecticut, he led a group of settlers who founded Newark, New Jersey;

PUTNAM

some time later he was commander in chief of the colonial forces in the long fight with the Indians known as King Philip's War. Also of historical interest is the large obelisk in red sandstone, erected in 1852 to the memory of forty-six Revolutionary soldiers who were set ashore in Milford from a British prison ship on January 1, 1777, sick with smallpox; and to the memory of Captain Stephen Stow of Milford, who volunteered to nurse the men and who died as a result. The inscription on this monument concludes, "Who shall say that Republics are ungrateful?"

There remain a few stones bearing legible seventeenth-century dates, together with a large number of stones from the whole of the eighteenth century. Note, among many good ones, the adjacent stones of the Reverend Samuel Whittelsey and his son, the former (d. 1768) in slate and in Latin, the latter (d. 1776) in red sandstone and in English. There is a fine epitaph on the stone of Jonah Newton, d. 1794 ae. 18. But everyone's favorite Milford epitaph is to be found on the last slate gravestone toward the southeast corner, by the tracks, above the grave of Miss Mary Fowler, d. 1792 ae. 24:

> Molly tho pleasant in her day
> Was sudd'nly seiz'd and sent away
> How soon shes ripe how soon shes rott'n
> Sent to her grave, & soon forgott'n

MOHEGAN

Fort Shantok Indian Burying Ground. [34]   In Fort Shantok
State Park, at the site of the fort. The road to Fort Shantok (so
marked) runs east from Route 32, ¾ mile north of Mohegan
village.

As is commonly the case with Indian burying grounds, too
little remains in the way of monuments to recommend this
site as a cemetery in itself. It is, however, part of an attractive
state park, with a fine view of the Thames River; and a visit
to the cemetery adds historical interest to a pleasant afternoon
excursion.

This burying ground of the Mohegan Indians is situated at
Fort Shantok, where in 1645 Uncas, sachem of the Mohegan
and friendly to the British, withstood a siege by the hostile
Narragansett. Uncas was finally relieved by British troops
sent from Saybrook under Lt. Leffingwell. Sadly, the old stones
in the graveyard are broken and illegible. Of the more recent
monuments, one marks the grave of Fidelia Fielding (1827–
1908), the last person to speak the Mohegan-Pequot language.

MYSTIC

Denison Cemetery. [35]   On Route 1, opposite the Mystic
Motor Inn.

Very small but relatively interesting, this plot was the private
cemetery of the noted Denison family. The first grave is that
of Captain John Denison, d. 1698 ae. 52. Many Denisons of
later generations were Revolutionary soldiers. There are
numerous interesting eighteenth-century stones.

NEW HAVEN

Grove Street Cemetery. [36] Grove Street. Open 7 A.M.–4:30 P.M. daily.

A large, formal cemetery laid out in 1797. It has a handsome, restrained appearance: the occasional exuberance of Victorian mortuary styles seems to have been kept at bay by the nononsense theology of neighboring Yale College. The entrance is marked by a massive brownstone "Egyptian Revival" gate, completed in 1848. This is one of several such gates in New England (there is one at Mt. Auburn, for instance); they represented the height of grandeur at the time of their construction.

A chart posted inside the gate gives the location of the graves of the many distinguished persons buried at Grove Street. Of these the most notable include Timothy Dwight, Eli Whitney, Noah Webster, Charles Goodyear, and Lyman Beecher, a liberal revivalist and the father of Henry Ward Beecher and Harriet Beecher Stowe.

In the northwest corner, leaning against the wall, are some four hundred stones moved here from an early burial ground on New Haven Green.

NEW LONDON

Antient Burying Ground. [37] Between Huntington and Hempstead Streets; the entrance is on Huntington Street.

A very old cemetery with a somewhat abandoned air about it, containing an excellent collection of seventeenth- and eighteenth-century stones. One of the very oldest and most interesting is a large red stone, flat in the ground, inscribed "An epitaph on Captain Richard Lord deceased / May 17

1662 aetatis suae 51. . . ." There follow eight lines of very agreeable verse with a pronounced metaphysical flavor, beginning

> The bright starre of our cavallrie lyes here
> Unto the State a counsellour full deare. . . .

Another serious epitaph of interest is on the stone of Captain Adam Shapley, "who bravely gave his Life for his Country a fatal Wound at Fort Griswold Sept. 6th 1781 caused his Death. . . ."

> Shapley, thy deed reverse
> the Common doom
> and make thy name
> immortal in a tomb.

Other distinguished men buried here include Curdon Saltonstall (d. 1724), a colonial governor of Connecticut; and, in a large tomb, Jonathan Brooks (1768–1848), "A boy patriot of the American Revolution."

N O R W I C H

Old Norwich Town Cemetery. [38]   In Norwichtown, north of Norwich proper; the cemetery is on Old Cemetery Lane, which runs from the junction of Town Street and Elm Avenue at the corner of Norwichtown Green.

A large cemetery comprised almost entirely of eighteenth-century stones, with a wide variety of carving styles. Near the entrance are two memorials to twenty French soldiers who died in Norwich during the Revolutionary War: they camped at Norwichtown, under the command of Lafayette, in 1778. One memorial is in English, one in French. In the large tomb of the numerous and distinguished Huntington family is buried Samuel Huntington (1731–96), who was a signer of the Declaration of Independence, president of the Continental Congress, and governor of Connecticut.

Those interested in styles of stonecutting should notice in particular the stones of Deacon Simon and Mrs. Lydia Huntington, directly east of the Huntington family tomb. These are badly worn but nevertheless remarkable specimens, especially the footstones, which are large, trapezoidal in shape, featuring a circular, abstract design with the names written around the circumference.

In the extreme northwest corner of the cemetery is a white marble stone reading:

> Alas poor human nature.
> In Memory of Mr
> B E N J A M I N   B U T L E R
> who died of a Phthisis
> pulmonaris June 17th AD
> 1787, in the 48th year
> of his age.

Poor human nature, having paid the doctor and paid for a stone, is unwilling to call it plain "consumption."

O L D   L Y M E

 Duck River Cemetery. [39]   On Shore Road, south of village center.

Pleasantly situated by a little river. The oldest plot contains the graves of five veterans of King Philip's War in the 1670's. Many Revolutionary soldiers are here, and several governors of Connecticut.

P U T N A M

Grove Street Cemetery. [40]   At the junction of Routes 12 and 52.

Near the northwest corner of this cemetery a solid granite monument marks the grave of Phineas G. Wright, d. 1918 ae. 89. A large bust in relief depicts Mr. Wright wearing a beard, a watch chain and a worried expression; beneath it a legend reads, "Going, But Know Not Where."

Old Killingly Burial Ground. [41]   On Route 12, ½ mile south of the village center.

The two cemeteries in Putnam make a pleasant contrast and a good combination: having paid his respects to Phineas G. Wright, the visitor may proceed to Old Killingly for some eighteenth-century verities. This peaceful cemetery, surrounded by a stone wall, was laid out in 1720; a plaque at the gate lists thirty-five Revolutionary veterans buried within. Among the old slates several are extremely well preserved and unusually beautiful in a simple, restrained style: note for instance those of the Larned family at the far side of the cemetery.

R I D G E F I E L D

Ridgefield Cemetery. [42]   On Route 116, one mile north of the village center.

A large cemetery with a variety of styles in a relatively peaceful suburban setting. In the center are some old stones dating back to the 1740's—note that of the Reverend Thomas Hawley, pastor of the village church. Elsewhere are some grand Victorian sculptures, and one rather modest stone from the mid-nineteenth century, in memory of the four sons of Elisha and Charity Hawley, "whose remains lie interred in various parts of the world," recounting where each of them died.

SAYBROOK POINT

Cypress Cemetery. [43]   Main Street (Route 154).

This pretty site overlooking the bay held, in the seventeenth century, the vital British fortification of the mouth of the Connecticut River. Near the road, enclosed by an iron railing, is the tomb of Lady Alice Fenwick (d. 1648), the wife of Col. George Fenwick, governor of Saybrook Fort. Having arrived from England to find that her life in the New World would be spent within the walls of a military fort, Lady Alice consoled herself by planting a garden of English flowers; according to Mrs. Abbot, "Merry Lady Alice was most often seen amidst her flowers singing blithely old madrigals."

One corner of the present cemetery consists of a square plot, empty except for a monument identifying it as the first site of Yale College. This ground was given to the town in 1914 on condition that it never be used for burials. The facts of the matter seem to be that this was the *second* site of Yale College, during the years 1707–1716: the institution was then known as "The Collegiate School of Connecticut." The Collegiate School had previously operated at Killingworth during the years 1702–1707. In 1716 it moved to New Haven, and in 1718 it was renamed in honor of its benefactor, Elihu Yale.

STONINGTON

Evergreen Cemetery. [44]   South side of Route 1, at North
Main Street.

Very large; the older section is of the nineteenth century and
contains several elaborate monuments in the grand Victorian
manner. Within this section is an area of somewhat older
graves, from the early nineteenth century. In the first row of
these, toward the south wall of the cemetery, are several
marble obelisks of medium size: one is of particular interest.
It stands in memory of the four sons of Amos and Hannah
Denison, and the four sides of the monument relate the way in
which each of the sons met his death:

—Ezra S. Denison, d. 1812 ae. 20, in the War of 1812, aboard
a privateer "off the Western Islands"

—Captain Amos Denison Jr., d. 1816 ae. 36, "swept from
the deck of the schooner, Nancy, on a voyage to the West
Indies"

—Captain Charles W. Denison, d. 1817 ae. 39, "who departed
this life at Paramaribo, Surinam"

—Edward Denison, d. 1818 ae. 28, "died at Balaria in India"

The lengthy epitaphs that follow include details of each man's
career.

Old Town Cemetery. [45]   On Broad Street, south of Water
Street.

A small, pleasant cemetery, neatly walled-in and almost
hidden from the street, with a view of the harbor. A large proportion of the stones tell of seafaring deaths: "Capt. Amos
Sheffield, who died at Demerara"; "Capt. James Sheffield, who
was drowned"; "Capt. Thomas Robinson who was drowned

near Point Judith"; "Franses W. Holmes . . . who died on his passage from Demerary to this port June 6th 1801: in Lat. 20—39′ N. & Long. 64. W. Aged 14 Years."

Wequetequock Burying Ground. [46]   In Wequetequock, east of Stonington: the cemetery lies just west of Greenhaven Road, which runs south from Route 1 at the traffic light.

The first cemetery in the town of Stonington. A large monument recounts the careers of four of the founders of the town in the mid-seventeenth century, all of whom are buried here: William Chesebrough, Lt. Thomas Minor, Walter Palmer, and Thomas Stanton. There are numerous legible stones from the eighteenth century: among many interesting ones note the double headstone of John and Mercy Breed, bearing an inscription headed, "In Memory of a pious pair."

STRATFORD

Christ Church Cemetery. [47]   Behind Christ Church (Episcopal) , on Main Street.

A small, historically interesting cemetery: it is kept locked, with the key available on request at the parsonage across Main Street from the church.

Christ Church in Stratford, established 1724, was the first Anglican church in Connecticut; its cemetery is accordingly the oldest Episcopal burying ground in the state. The chief historical interest of the cemetery consists in the graves of Samuel Johnson and William Samuel Johnson, father and son, two of the first presidents of what is now Columbia University.

Samuel Johnson was born in Guilford, Connecticut in 1696—thirteen years before the birth of the English author. He was the founder of Christ Church in Stratford and in 1756 became the first president of

King's College (later Columbia), a newly founded Anglican institution. Johnson corresponded with George Berkeley, the English philosopher, and was the foremost American exponent of Berkeley's philosophical idealism—commonly known as the doctrine which maintains that a tree in the woods does not exist unless there is someone there to see it. Johnson died in 1772. His son, William Samuel Johnson (1727–1819), was a leading figure in the public life of Connecticut: in spite of the fact that he opposed the independence of the American colonies, he was elected to the Continental Congress in 1774. Johnson refused to serve. But in 1787, presented with a *fait accompli,* he played an important part in the Constitutional Convention; he was then made president of the renamed Columbia College. In 1789 he was elected U.S. senator from Connecticut, but he retained a certain diffidence about the job: when the federal capital was moved in 1791 from New York to Philadelphia, Johnson declined to commute and resigned.

It is said that the weathercock on the spire of Christ Church still bears bullet holes from potshots taken by British soldiers quartered here in the 1750's. This interesting assertion is impossible to confirm with the naked eye from street level.

TERRYVILLE

Eastchurch Cemetery. [48]   On East Plymouth Road. Drive ¾ mile north on Route 72 from Route 6; bear right at the small "package" store; follow East Plymouth Road to the cemetery by the abandoned church in the village of East Plymouth.

A simple cemetery, quiet and isolated, of nineteenth-century date: it has the attractions of a place which modern settlements have largely left behind.

The peaceful rows of marble gravestones do not show it, but many of the citizens buried here made up a hotbed of Toryism during the Revolutionary War. Prominent among them, and buried in the first row, were Stephen and Ruth Graves. When patriots were seen in the neighborhood, out on a Tory raid, Ruth would blow on a conch shell to sound the alarm. Stephen Graves and his cohorts would hide in a local cave known as the Tory Den.

TRUMBULL

Unity Burial Ground. [49]   On Unity Road, off Route 127, just south of the Merritt Parkway.

This small graveyard dates from 1730. It contains a number of interesting old stones, in good condition, in both slate and red sandstone.

WALLINGFORD

Center Cemetery. [50]   On Center Street, west of Main Street.

A large, walled-in cemetery in the center of Wallingford; unfortunately, the oldest stones can no longer be seen and it is not as interesting as it might be. Of the few eighteenth-century stones that remain, several bear a highly stylized "portrait" in profile, interesting because such different people, male and female, are represented so nearly alike. A white marble slab atop a tomb of red sandstone marks what was at one time thought to be the final resting place of the Hon. Lyman Hall (d. 1790), a signer of the Declaration of Independence, a Governor of Connecticut, and later a Governor of Georgia. Hall was born in Wallingford and buried in Wallingford, but a delegation from Georgia removed his remains and reinterred them in Augusta.

WATERBURY

East Farms Cemetery. [51]   At the far eastern end of town, behind the house at 3156 East Main Street. A grassy path leads to the cemetery between two private houses.

This small cemetery, set far back from the road, is not difficult to find when you know how; but its seclusion and its unexpected position make it a happy discovery. East Farms Cemetery has been a town burying ground since 1780. A handful of the old stones remain; there are graves of Revolutionary and other veterans.

A large granite monument, erected in 1914 by public subscription, marks the graves of two anonymous French soldiers of the army of Rochambeau, who died here in 1781 while en route from Newport to Yorktown to fight under Washington.

WETHERSFIELD

Ancient Burying Ground. [52]   Behind the Congregational Church, at Main and Marsh Streets in the center of the village.

The old cemetery at Wethersfield starts immediately behind the church and rises up and over a hill to the back: it covers a large area and the whole of it is crowded with stones. It is most impressive by the sheer number of surviving seventeenth- and eighteenth-century stones, primarily red and brown. The early settlers of Wethersfield, who were among the first white men in Connecticut, are buried here; and there is evidence of Indian burials as well.

Some of the most interesting monuments are among the impressive group of table stones at the top of the hill. The oldest stone of all, that of Leonard Chester, Armiger (d. 1648), is decorated with a very rough approximation of the dragons on the Chester coat of arms. Another table stone nearby was evidently begun as a monument exclusively for Col. Elisha Williams, with a long and glorious epitaph. At a later time, one corner was marked off to commemorate his first wife, Eunice: it contains a glowing epitaph somewhat limited by space. Finally a second corner was allotted to his second wife, Elizabeth. This corner is inset with a slate tablet, which carries a laudatory epitaph written very small.

WILTON

Sharp Hill Burying Ground. [53]   On Route 7 at the corner of Sharp Hill Road: south of the town hall.

Small and semi-derelict; not worth a detour, but worth a stop. A few eighteenth-century stones remain in good condition, and among these are several of interest. There are graves of many Revolutionary soldiers.

Ye Old God's Acre. [54]   Route 7, next to the town hall.

The name of this cemetery is inscribed on an ornamental gate dated 1890. The stones within are of the mid-nineteenth century or later, most of them of no particular interest. What is striking here is the setting: a narrow lot, leading far back up a hill, with stone walls on either side and a grassy path up the middle, offering a very inviting walk. Halfway up this path, to the right, note the marble stone of "Our Little Mary," d. 1858. It bears an extraordinary engraved medallion figure of which the design, comprised of roses and scrollwork, combines to make a face: seen today, the effect is that of a crude caricature of a person weeping. This curious design is found on other stones in the town, but not so well preserved as this example.

WINDHAM

Old Burying Ground. [55]   On Route 203, ¾ mile south of Windham village.

Unusually extensive, with a very large number of eighteenth-century slate stones. Many are worn and difficult to read, but the interesting variety of the stonecutting makes a visit worthwhile. Notice for instance several examples of an unusual style found in this area: stones decorated with a round face in high relief (i.e., convex), surrounded by wings on either side incised in the ordinary manner. Two large additions to the cemetery hold nineteenth- and twentieth-century graves.

WINDSOR

Palisado Cemetery. [56]   On Palisado Avenue (Route 159), behind the Congregational Church, northeast of the village center.

Far behind the church, beyond the modern cemetery, is the old graveyard of the town of Windsor, one of the earliest settlements in Connecticut. The first settlers are buried here, along with many eminent citizens of later times. The Mather family is particularly well represented; the marker of Timothy Mather, M.D. (d. 1788) is one of the largest pieces of red sandstone to be seen anywhere.

The prize stone here, considered to be the oldest extant in Connecticut, forms part of the low tomb of the Rev. Ephraim Huit (d. 1644), "sometimes teacher to the church of Windsor." His brief epitaph is one of the select few, anywhere in New England, that can justifiably be called poetry.

> who when hee lived, we drew our vitall breath
> who when hee dyed, his dying was our death

who was the stay of State the Churches Staff
Alas the times forbides an Epitaph

WOODSTOCK

Woodstock Hill Cemetery. [57]   On Route 169, next to the First Congregational Church at the end of the village green.

The old churchyard in this attractive village has a beautiful hillside setting looking over the Thompson Hills in the distance. It is well kept and contains some fine old stones. The most notable monument here is, however, a relatively new one. The back of the Frink family stone, a large piece of polished granite not far from the road, is inscribed in memory of Ethal Barrett (d. 1941). On one side of the Frink/Barrett monument is a cameo portrait of Barrett posed with a dog, a gun, and a fox. The legend reads, "This is Fanny, my favorite fox hound. I have shot over two hundred foxes with the gun that I hold."

MAINE

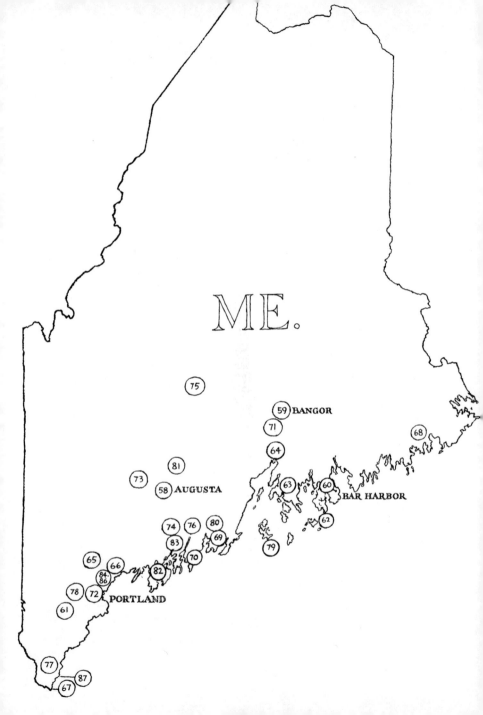

ME.

58. Augusta
59. Bangor
60. Bar Harbor
61. Bar Mills
62. Bernard
63. Blue Hill
64. Bucksport   72. Portland
65. Gray   73. Readfield
66. Harpswell Center 74. Richmond
67. Kittery Point 75. Ripley
68. Machias   76. Sheepscott
69. Medomak   77. South Berwick
70. New Harbor 78. South Windham
71. Orrington   79. Vinalhaven
        80. Waldoboro
        81. Winslow
        82. Wiscasset
        83. Woolwich
       84–86. Yarmouth
        87. York

SOUTH WINDHAM

As soon

Seek roses in December—ice in

June;

Hope constancy in wind, or corn

in chaff;

Believe a woman or an epi-

taph. . . .

LORD BYRON

AUGUSTA

Hallowell Cemetery. [58]   On Water Street (Route 201), a short distance south of the State House.

At the back of this large, nineteenth-century cemetery is an old section which contains several interesting things. A number of the stones are decorated with an unusual pattern of wavy lines: the best example is the large slate of Nathaniel Shaw (d. 1801), almost hidden by a huge maple tree. In the same row, not far away, a stone tells the following story: "In memory of Peter Clark, who left his home, May 7, 1797 aged 62 y'rs and perished in the wilderness; his remains were found Sept. 11, 1803 and intered here." The gravestone of Obadiah Harris (d. 1800), a Deacon of the first church in Hallowell, shows a fine grapevine design. And the handsome slate of Mrs. Lucy Gow (d. 1805 ae. 30) carries in its epitaph a much stronger dose of doctrine than usual:

> Blame not the monumental stone we raise,
> T'is to the Saviour's, not the sinner's, praise.
> Sin was the whole, that she could call her own,
> Her good was all derived from him alone.
> To sin, her conflicts, pains, & griefs she ow'd,
> Her conquering faith & patience, he bestowed.
> Reader, mayst thou obtain like precious faith,
> To smile in anguish and rejoice in death.

B A N G O R

Mount Hope Cemetery. [59]   On State Street (Route 2), two miles north of the city center.

Mount Hope was designed expressly to be an imitation Mount Auburn. It falls short of the model in most respects, but the Bangor cemetery has some attractive features of its own. The most interesting monuments are within a short distance of the entrance gate.

The striking bronze sculpture that catches the eye by the entrance is in fact, rarity of rarities, a *modern* Civil War memorial. Mount Hope has a conventional Civil War memorial (built in 1864) not far away; this one, to be specific, is a memorial to the Second Maine Regiment of Volunteers. Funds for its construction and maintenance were left in a bequest by Col. Luther Peirce, a native of Bangor and a member of the Second Maine. Col. Peirce died in 1915, but various complications delayed the erection of the memorial until 1963. The pleasing and paradoxical result is that, instead of yet another statue of a Union soldier at attention, the Second Maine has for its memorial an interesting modern sculpture which may even cause passersby to think for a moment about the Civil War. The legend, taken from one of John Greenleaf Whittier's abolitionist poems, is "Not painlessly doth God recast and mold anew the Nation."

To the north of the entrance, near the road, is the tomb of Hannibal Hamlin (1809–91), who served as Vice President under Lincoln. Near the main driveway (surmounted by a ball of polished granite) is the grave of James Peavey, a famous lumberman. Peavey was the inventor of the lumberman's log handling tool known as a peavey (or, according to the dictionary, as a peavy, peevy, or pevy: the variety of names is evidence of its universal acceptance). A small drawing of a peavey is engraved on the stone. Another grave of particular interest cannot easily be located. This is the unmarked grave of Mr. Al Brady.

For a brief period in 1937, Al Brady was Public Enemy Number One on the official list kept by the FBI. With an associate, Clarence Shaffer, Jr., Brady came to Bangor: their intention was to lie low for a while and—in a casual, offhand manner—to order some replacement machine gun parts. They did not manage to do so without attracting attention. One day in October, 1937, the two men were apprehended and shot to death outside Dakin's Sporting Goods store, then located on Central Street. Shaffer's body was claimed by relatives. Brady was buried in Mount Hope Cemetery, but no monument was provided.

BAR HARBOR

 Old Town Cemetery. [60]   On Mt. Desert Street, between the Congregational and Episcopal churches.

Small, neat, and orderly, seasoned with the graves of several old sea captains. The stone of Capt. James Hamor has a medallion in relief showing a ship in very rough seas, perhaps about to be wrecked. The cemetery is dominated by a huge Civil War monument.

BAR MILLS

Tory-Hill Meeting House Yard. [61]   In the town of Buxton, at the junction of routes 112 and 4A.

The Tory-Hill Meeting House itself is a famous old church, well worth visiting. Its churchyard is now just the corner of a huge modern cemetery; even so it appears small, quiet, and very beautiful. None of the stones are old enough to be particularly interesting in themselves. But the combination of appropriate stones, tall trees, and a handsome church building, makes this shady corner a pleasant stopping place.

BERNARD

Bernard Cemetery. [62]   On Route 102, just south of the turn-off to the village.

Those who are assiduous in the collecting of recognized oddities or cemeteries with literary associations may wish, for the sake of completeness, to make the trip to Bernard. Otherwise it cannot be recommended.

Elias Rich (d. 1867) was a local ne'er-do-well, known to the townsfolk for his fervent belief in the glories of the life that awaited him in the hereafter. Some time after his death a pattern began to appear in the marble of his gravestone which was held by many to resemble the features of their late neighbor; and the lines that continued to emerge appeared to depict a "heavenly crown" on his head. Elias ("Heavenly Crown") Rich became a local legend. The story was used as the basis

of a poem by Holman Day, published in *Pine Tree Ballads*
(1902). The following is a brief excerpt:

> Friends placed above Elias' grave a plain, white marble
>   stone,
> And months went by. Then all at once 'twas seen that
>   there had grown
> Upon the polished marble slab a shading that, 'twas said,
> Took on a shape extremely like Elias' shaggy head.
> Then soon above the shadowy brows a crown was slowly
>   limned,
> And though Aunt Rich scrubbed zealously the thing could
>   not be dimmed.

The trouble with all this, of course, is that it now takes a very
lively imagination indeed to recognize anything like a human
head on the Elias Rich stone, let alone a "heavenly crown."
Presumably, additional markings in the stone have emerged
to spoil the clarity of the apparition.

BLUE HILL

The Old Cemetery. [63]   On Union Street (Route 177), west
of the village center.

Small, isolated, shaded by many trees; there are several interesting stones. The epitaph of Deacon Simeon Parker (d.
1826) is nicely phrased:

> Sustained by grace to bear afflictions well,
> In life's meridian, but mature, he fell.

BUCKSPORT

Buck Cemetery. [64]   On Main Street (combined Routes 1, 3, and 15) 150 yards east of the Verona Bridge.

This small and agreeable cemetery is, most regrettably, kept locked; but the reason for its fame is clearly visible from outside the fence. One side of the large granite monument to the town's eponym, Col. Jonathan Buck, appears to show the black outline of a woman's high-buttoned, pointed-toed boot. Several efforts were made to sand away the mark, but each time it returned. The story is that in his early life, before coming to Maine, Col. Buck executed a woman accused of being a witch; and that the mark on his monument is the trace of her curse. Of course, if such is the case, it would appear that the woman really *was* a witch: thus the mark becomes a further tribute to the Colonel's perspicacity.

GRAY

Gray Cemetery. [65]   Behind the firehouse, in the center of the village.

There are some interesting old stones in this large cemetery: near the firehouse, note the very large and extraordinary slate at the grave of the Freemason Russell Bucknam, "who departed this life August 13, A.L. 5806: AEt. 31." The stone bears a variety of symbolic carvings.

   The most famous grave in Gray may be found along the sixth driveway, counting from the back of the firehouse. During the Civil War, a coffin arrived in Gray, sent from one of the battlefields: it was found to contain the body of a Confederate soldier. The unknown Southerner was buried beneath a plain marble tablet reading

> STRANGER
> A Soldier
> of the late war
> died 1862
> Erected
> by the Ladies of Gray.

On Memorial Day, amid a field of miniature stars and stripes, this one grave is marked by a Confederate flag.

HARPSWELL CENTER

Old Common Cemetery. [66]   On Route 123, across from the Congregational Church.

A small graveyard of very attractive simplicity. The earliest stones date from the late eighteenth century. Among these is a fine slate marker for the first pastor of the church across the road, the Rev. Elisha Eaton, "who triumphantly departed this life" in 1764. As an epitaph, a familiar admonition has been made into a jingle:

> Est commune mori,
> Mors nulli Parcit Honori,
> Neque ulli Aetati,
> Ergo, MEMENTO MORI.

Next to the church itself is a monument to another of its pastors, Elijah Kellogg (1813–1901), who was widely known as a writer of popular stories for boys. Kellogg's most famous work was the recitation piece, "Spartacus to the Gladiators."

K I T T E R Y   P O I N T

Old Burying Yard. [67]   On Route 103, by the river, across
the road from the Congregational Church.

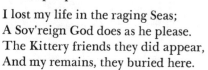

The small graveyard in Kittery Point combines a very attractive setting with a disproportionate share of interesting and
unusual monuments. The most famous stone stands in the
high grass just beyond the southwest corner of the cemetery
proper. This is the gravestone of Margaret Hills (d. 1803, ae.
28), with its noted epitaph:

> I lost my life in the raging Seas;
> A Sov'reign God does as he please.
> The Kittery friends they did appear,
> And my remains, they buried here.

In the same corner, though within the area that is kept mowed,
is the grave of Levi Lincoln Thaxter (d. 1885). Thaxter's
wife, Celia Thaxter, was a New Hampshire poetess, perhaps
best known for her *Drift-Weed* (1879): on his death, she commissioned an epitaph from Robert Browning, explaining that
her late husband had always been particularly fond of Browning's verse. The resulting poem is a very graceful piece of
work, considering the difficulties of writing an epitaph for a
man one has never met. It was originally inscribed on a fieldstone, later copied on a bronze plaque which was affixed to
the stone. The epitaph concludes:

> I gave but of the little that I knew:
> How were the gift requited, while along
> Life's path I pace, couldst thou make weakness strong:
> Help me with knowledge—for life's old, death's new.

At the other end of the cemetery is another interesting stone: once again it is in the corner, down a little path into the high grass by the Piscataqua River. Recently carved in black slate, it bears a medallion engraving of a shipwreck, with the small figure of a desperate victim visible on the deck. The inscription is as follows:

Brig 'Hattie Eaton'
W. I. to Boston
Cast away on Gerrish
Island Mch 21, 1876
Crew of 8, white and
negro, and 1 stowaway.
Near this stone lie six
bodies never claimed.

MACHIAS

O'Brien Cemetery. [68]   Off Elm Street, on a hill overlooking the Machias River.

An attractive cemetery on a particularly handsome site. Here are buried the seventeenth-century founders of Machias and the heroes of the town's greatest exploit—the Battle of the *Margaretta.*

It is not generally known (outside Washington County, Maine) that the first naval battle of the Revolution took place on the Machias River. It was on this wise. In June of 1775 the British were increasing the strength of their troops in America. The King's loyal subjects in the town of Machias were ordered to supply lumber for additional barracks being built in Boston. The townsfolk met to discuss this demand, standing by the banks of the small stream which runs just to the east of the O'Brien Cemetery. Men of revolutionary

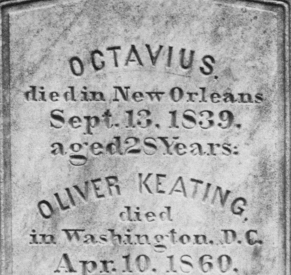

OCTAVIUS,
died in New Orleans
Sept. 13, 1839,
aged 28 Years:

OLIVER KEATING,
died
in Washington, D.C.
Apr. 10, 1860,
aged 54 Years:

GEORGE,
died on board Steam Ship.
Aug. 1861,
on the passage from
San Francisco to New York,
aged 59 Years:

JOSEPH,
died in Salmon Falls, Cal.
July 1, 1862,
aged 54 Years:

sons of
Jonathan S. & Mary Barrell
of York, Me.

sentiments, notably Jeremiah O'Brien and Benjamin Foster, urged that the British demand be rejected. At length Foster delivered an impassioned speech and jumped across the stream, inviting all fellow rebels to join him: eventually everyone did so, and the stream was thereafter named "Foster's Rubicon." Word of the rebellion reached the British, who sent the armed schooner *Margaretta* up the Machias River to enforce the order about supplying lumber. On June 12, 1775, the men of Machias commandeered a small boat and attacked the *Margaretta*, killing its commander and capturing the ship.

M E D O M A K

 Bremen Town Cemetery. [69]   In the Town of Bremen; on Route 32, just south of the road leading to the village of Medomak.

A modest roadside cemetery. The attractive older section lies on the east side of the road; a modern section, currently in use, is opposite. The setting is quiet and pleasant, enclosed by a stone wall and surrounded by woods. The one really remarkable feature is the handsome statue of Commander Samuel Tucker (1747–1833), "Patriot of the Revolution," erected in his memory by the State of Maine.

Samuel Tucker was commissioned a privateer by George Washington in the Revolutionary War: his officially-sanctioned depredations on British vessels earned him great renown and a pension (by Act of Congress) of $20 a month. Tucker's enduring reputation rests on two things: the statue in Bremen, and a mention in the Diaries of John Adams. When Adams was appointed commissioner to France in February, 1778, he sailed with Tucker from Marblehead to Bordeaux. In his account of the voyage there is this note:

> Our Captn. is an able Seaman, and a brave, active, vigilant officer, but I believe has no great Erudition. His Library consists of Dyche's English Dictionary, Charlevoix's Paraguay, The Rights of

the Xtian Church asserted vs. the Romish and other Priests, who claim an independent Power over it, The 2d Vol. of Chubbs posthumous Works, 1. Vol. of the History of Charles Horton, Esq. and 1 Vol. of the delicate Embarrassments a Novell.—I shall at some other Time take more Notice of some of these Books.

A few days later, Tucker made Adams a present of Charlevoix's *Paraguay*. The book remains in the Adams library to this day.

NEW HARBOR

Fort William Henry Cemetery. [70] A road marked to the Fort runs west from Route 130 from a point just north of the village of New Harbor.

Fort William Henry, in a state of very partial restoration, occupies a pretty site on a piece of land jutting into the cove. The Fort itself was very extensive, including paved streets, but very short-lived: it was built in 1692 and destroyed by the French in 1696. Such artifacts as have been discovered are displayed in a museum. The small cemetery at the site contains a number of interesting eighteenth-century stones, most of them carved of imported Welsh slate.

ORRINGTON

Village Cemetery. [71] On Route 15, south of the village center, approximately opposite the post office.

A nineteenth-century cemetery of moderate interest. In a fenced-off family plot is a marble obelisk in memory of George A. Wentworth, who "was captured on Wilson's raid June 29, and died a prisoner at Andersonville, N.C. Sept. 6, 1864, AE. 20 yrs. . . ." (Andersonville was actually in Georgia; compare the famous Andersonville stone in St. Albans, Vt.) The Wentworth monument, as do several in this cemetery, contains a niche to hold a tintype of the deceased: in this case, the tintype is still there and can still (though just barely) be made out. Elsewhere in the cemetery are many graves of sea captains, some decorated with figures of ships and anchors, some with epitaphs describing deaths at sea; as for instance Capt. Thomas Atwood, "Lost in the Brig Neptune with all on board between Amsterdam and N. York Oct. 1818."

PORTLAND

Eastern Cemetery. [72]   On Congress Street, just north of its intersection with Route 1A; in an old section of the city, north of the center. Congress Street bends around and runs for a long way to the west of the city: do not follow it in this direction.

Eastern Cemetery lies in a state of mild decay amid mildly decayed surroundings: it overlooks Portland Harbor, filled with oil tankers. Established before 1700, it was for two centuries the only burial place within the City of Portland. As a result it is overcrowded, and it offers a great deal to look at.

The most notable graves here are of a number of naval heroes of the early nineteenth century. Most easily spotted is the large marble monument to Commodore Edward Preble (1761–1807), who was chosen by Jefferson to lead the American fleet against the Barbary pirates in the Tripolitan War. Preble's flagship was the U.S.S. *Constitution,* later known as "Old Ironsides." The Commodore having scored several noted victories over the infidel pirates, Pope Pius VII declared that Preble had "done more for Christianity in a short space of

time than the most powerful nations have done in ages." Some
distance to the southeast is the grave of Lt. Henry Wadsworth,
an uncle of the poet Longfellow; the white marble marker is
unfortunately virtually illegible. Wadsworth, a twenty-year-
old naval officer, was killed off Tripoli when his ship, the
Intrepid, was blown up to save it from capture—during the
Barbary campaign led by Preble.

Next to the Wadsworth stone are the most interesting of all
these naval monuments. Side by side are three brick tombs,
topped with marble slabs. Two of these cover the graves of the
commanders of the opposing sides of one of the decisive naval
battles of the War of 1812: Lt. William Burrowes, aged twenty-
eight, who commanded the U.S. brig *Enterprise,* and Capt.
Samuel Blyth, aged twenty-nine, commander of the British
brig *Boxer.* The two men fought each other and were killed in
action September 5, 1813. The victorious *Enterprise* arrived in
Portland two days later with the captured British ship. The
bodies of the two young commanders were taken ashore in
ten-oared barges, amid cannon salutes and a funeral procession
of all the ships in the harbor. The stones are beautifully engraved. Burrowes' tablet notes that it was erected by "a passing
stranger," while Blyth's was erected by "the surviving officers
of his crew." The third of the three tombs marks the grave of
Lt. Kervin Waters, aged eighteen, a midshipman aboard the
Enterprise; it was erected by "the young men of Portland."
Longfellow, who was a boy in Portland at the time, recalled
the scene in a stanza of his poem, "My Lost Youth":

> I remember the sea-fight far away,
> > How it thundered o'er the tide!
> And the dead captains, as they lay
> > In their graves, o'erlooking the tranquil bay,
> > Where they in battle died.

READFIELD

Monk's Hill Cemetery. [73]   East of Route 17, just north of the Readfield/Manchester town line.

On a quiet hillside near Lake Cobbosseecontee. There are graves of the early Baptist settlers of the area. Prominent among these is the tomb of Elder Isaac Case, born in 1761, "converted to the christian religion" in 1779, who "gathered a church" in Readfield in 1792 and was its pastor until 1800. There are some interesting old slates: the oldest and best is a double headstone for a brother and sister, Ebenezer and Rusha Monk, d. 1789 ae. 9 and 4, respectively. A small slate marks the grave of Charles Fuller, d. 1816 ae. 3 years 7 months: "his death was occasioned by the kick of a horse." Next to this is the stone of his mother, who had died within a month of his birth.

RICHMOND

Richmond Cemetery. [74]   On Route 197, west of the village.

In the section next to the road, this is a perfectly ordinary New England cemetery of nineteenth-century vintage. Further back is a large area of stones marked in Cyrillic characters, marked with or shaped like Russian Orthodox crosses. Richmond, an old shipbuilding town on the Kennebec River, contains a large emigré colony of White Russians: one result is this interesting polyglot cemetery.

RIPLEY

West Ripley Cemetery. [75]   At Todd's Corner, on Route
154; a short distance west of the junction with Route 152.

The main attraction of West Ripley Cemetery is to those who
enjoy bizarre epitaphs. On the east side of this small graveyard
is a large monument to John L. Jones (1811–75) : on one side,
cut ineffaceably in granite, are three stanzas of cheerful
atheistic doggerel:

> I came without my own consent,
> Liv'd a few years much discontent,
>> At human errors grieving;
> I rul'd myself by reason's laws,
> But got contempt and not applause,
>> Because of disbelieving.

Those who would have the rest of it must go to Ripley.

SHEEPSCOTT

Sheepscott Cemetery. [76]   Just south of the village center:
take "The King's Highway" uphill, opposite the post office.

A small cemetery with no distinguished monuments but offering a particularly beautiful and peaceful setting. It stands on a
hilltop above the village, with a view of the head of the bay
beneath. Stones date from the eighteenth century to the present, including some good old ones.

SOUTH BERWICK

Oldfields Cemetery. [77]   On Vine Street, south of the village, in the vicinity known as Oldfields.

In a secluded, wooded setting, on a hill overlooking a pond. This old cemetery was restored some years ago, but not too much: there is still a pleasant feeling of discovering something hidden. It is surprisingly extensive; many of the stones are partially covered, out of sight of the road. There is a large number of eighteenth-century stones. All in all, a nice place to poke around in.

SOUTH WINDHAM

Smith-Anderson Cemetery. [78]   A lane leading to the cemetery, marked by a sign, begins opposite the Parson Smith House on River Road. This point on River Road is 2½ miles east of Route 4.

A most attractive cemetery, extremely isolated: the visitor who manages to get here is rewarded with a pleasing sense of discovery. In former times it boasted two massive tombs erected by the Anderson family, but the older and more elaborate of these has been broken into and destroyed. There are many attractive stones among the simpler monuments.

VINALHAVEN

John Carver Cemetery. [79]   On High Street, next to Shields Grocery.

This small island cemetery contains surprisingly elaborate monuments. Vinalhaven in former times had its own granite quarry, and the cemetery comprises a kind of exhibit of the local stone. The sloping ground is divided into terraced plots, each one set off by a curb built of yet more granite. The attractive setting overlooks the inlet known as Carver's Pond.

WALDOBORO

German Protestant Cemetery. [80]   On a hill behind the German Meeting House, south of the village on Route 32.

Waldoboro was settled by German immigrants who were encouraged to come by General Samuel Waldo, who happened to own the land. A marble obelisk, well to the back of the cemetery and next to the road, is inscribed, "This town was settled in 1748, by Germans, who emigrated to this place with the promise and expectation of finding a populous city, instead of which they found nothing but a wilderness. . . ."

The Meeting House itself is in excellent condition; it bears a plaque identifying it as one of the three oldest churches in Maine. The oldest gravestones, which stood nearby, have unfortunately been removed. It is said that they line the cellar of a certain house in the vicinity. Those that remain still include a number of interesting inscriptions. The stone of Lowell Brock, a Civil War soldier, notes that "He was taken prisoner by the Rebels, at Fair Play Md., July 10, 1863. No tidings have been received of him since." Not far away is the stone of Elizabeth M., wife of Capt. Silas N. Castner, "who died at sea on board Brig Peerless April 4, 1853, and was buried in Lat. 27° 20′ N. Long. 74° 50′ W. while on her passage from Boston to Havana AE. 27 yrs, 4 mos."

WINSLOW

Fort Hill Cemetery. [81]   On Halifax Street (Route 100A).

An attractive hillside setting; one stone bears a famous epitaph. Beneath an oak tree in the older section is the grave of Richard Thomas, d. 1824 ae. 75:

<blockquote>
An inglishman by birth,
A Whig of 76,
By occupation a cooper,
Now food for worms.
Like an old rum puncheon
marked, numbered and shooked,
He will be raised again
and finished by his creator.
</blockquote>

WISCASSET

Ancient Cemetery. [82]   On Federal Street (Route 218).

An exceptionally attractive old cemetery, surrounded by a white picket fence, with a view of the bay. The graveyard was laid out in 1735: the stone of Joshua Pool, dated 1739, remains in excellent condition. Nearby is an obelisk monument to the Hon. Samuel Sewall (d. 1814), Chief Justice of the Supreme Court of the Commonwealth, with a long and highly laudatory epitaph in Latin. (The "Commonwealth," of course, referred to Massachusetts; Maine did not become a separate state until

1820.) Near the center, note the very fine adjacent marble stones of Manasseh and Hannah Smith, his engraved with a sun, hers with a moon. In the far corner are two particularly interesting stones: that of Col. David Payson (d. 1814), with elaborate symbolism, and that of Mr. Thomas Woodman, "who died on his passage from Damarara to this Port Sept. 14th 1796 AEtat 52," with the epitaph,

> In foreign climes, alas! resigns his breath,
> His friends far from him in the hour of death.

W O O L W I C H

Denny Cemetery. [83] The cemetery is in Arrowsic Town, not in Woolwich at all; but you have to start at Woolwich to get there. Follow Route 127 for 4.65 miles south of Route 1. At this point Ball Head Road (unmarked) crosses Route 127 at a diagonal. Take the fork to the right. (If you cross the bridge to Georgetown, you have gone past Ball Head Road.) On Ball Head Road you will quickly come to a fork in the road. Go straight on. After another ¾ mile is another fork. Take the left-hand fork, and continue 1⅓ miles. Look for the cemetery in the woods on your right. If you come out into a clearing with a view of the water, you have gone a little too far.

Denny Cemetery is included as a suggested excursion for the adventuresome. In itself, it is a small cemetery containing a handful of attractive eighteenth-century stones. In context, it is an excellent example of a cemetery as an archaeological resource. Denny Cemetery is large enough (and the stones are expensive enough) to indicate that it was, 250 years ago, the center of a thriving settlement. As may be gathered from the directions, it is now a long way from anywhere. It is not, however, abandoned: graves of veterans have been marked by American flags.

YARMOUTH

Baptist Cemetery. [84]   On Hill Street, next to the old Baptist Church; from West Main Street (Route 115), a sign directs vistors uphill to the "Old Meeting House."

The stones of this cemetery (established 1796) are a rather ordinary nineteenth-century assortment. The attraction lies almost entirely in the setting, next to and behind an extremely handsome white frame church, enclosed by a white picket fence. Taken together it is a charming location. The church itself is open to visitors from 2–4 P.M. on Wednesdays during July and August.

Ledge Cemetery. [85]   On Route 88 at Gilman Road.

"The Ledge" has a beautiful situation and is beautifully kept up. Along the road is a white rail fence; on the far side is a stone wall; beyond that is an open field and a view of the inlet known as Broad Cove. The cemetery dates from 1770; it contains an interesting assortment of eighteenth- and nineteenth-century stones. A brief walk brings the visitor to the Pioneers' Burial Ground, just up the road.

Pioneers' Burial Ground. [86]   On Gilman Road, within sight of the Ledge Cemetery, which stands at the junction with Route 88.

Established 1731, the oldest graveyard in town. It is a small plot of land, carefully preserved, containing the graves of early settlers and Indian fighters—men who "defended the town against the savage enemies," according to a plaque in the middle. The collection of old stones makes an excellent antiquarian annex to the Ledge Cemetery, a hundred yards down the road.

YORK

Old York Cemetery. [87]   On Route 1A, opposite the Congregational Church.

Its combination of a classic New England setting and numerous interesting stones makes this one of the most attractive cemeteries in Maine. It is enclosed by a stone wall and beautifully kept; the collection of old slates is extraordinarily fine.

The most famous grave in York lies toward the back of the cemetery. Between the head- and footstones of Mrs. Mary Nasson (d. 1774, ae. 29) is a huge boulder filling the entire length of the grave. In later times the story came to be told that Mrs. Nasson had been executed for witchcraft, and the stone placed on her grave to keep her from climbing out. One of the obvious objections to this fabrication is that the headstone is an elaborate portrait stone, which it is unlikely anyone would have commissioned for the grave of a condemned witch. Other notable stones include the immense and elaborate slate of Jonathan Sayward (d. 1797), a tiny, rough "homemade" stone dated 1769, and near the road, a piece of New England iconography: a stone in memory of the four sons of the Barrell family, all dead far from home.

MASSACHUSETTS

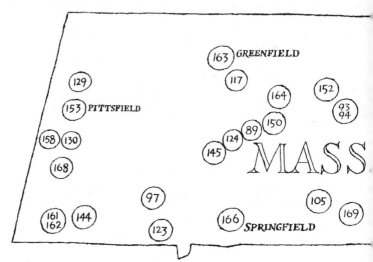

88. Amesbury
89. Amherst
90. Arlington
91, 92. Barnstable
93, 94. Barre
95, 96. Beverly
97. Blandford
98–103. Boston
104. Boxford
105. Brimfield
106. Burlington
107, 108. Cambridge
109. Chelmsford
110–112. Concord
113, 114. Danvers
115, 116. Dedham
117. Deerfield
118, 119. Duxbury
120. Fall River
121. Falmouth
122. Foxboro

123. Granville
124. Hadley
125. Harvard
126. Haverhill
127. Ipswich
128. Lakeville
129. Lanesboro
130. Lenox
131. Leominster
132. Lexington
133. Lowell
134. Manchester
135. Marblehead
136. Marlborough
137. Marshfield
138. Martha's Vineyard
139. Middleboro
140. Milton
141. Nantucket
142, 143. Newburyport
144. New Marlboro

145. Northampton
146, 147. North
        Andover
148. Northborough
149. North Reading
150. Pelham
151. Pepperell
152. Petersham
153. Pittsfield
154. Plymouth
155. Provincetown
156. Quincy
157. Rehoboth
158. Richmond
159. Salem
160. Sandwich
161, 162. Sheffield
163. Shelburne
164. Shutesbury
165. South Chelmsford
166. Springfield

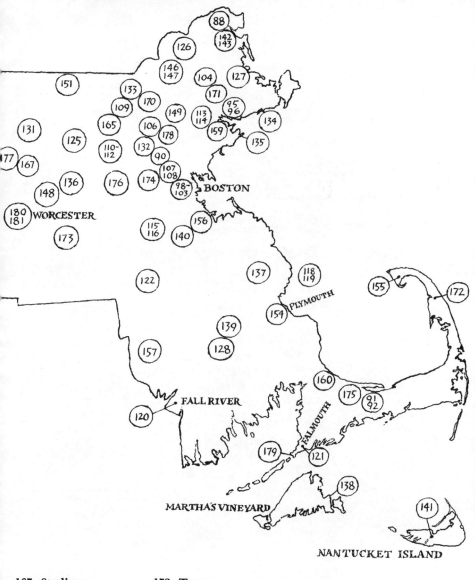

167. Sterling
168. Stockbridge
169. Sturbridge
170. Tewksbury
171. Topsfield

172. Truro
173. Upton
174. Watertown
175. West Barnstable
176. Weston

177. West Sterling
178. Woburn
179. Woods Hole
180. 181. Worcester

DUXBURY

*The stones in this wilderness are
already grown so witty as to
speak.*

COTTON MATHER (1693)

AMESBURY

Union Cemetery. [88]   On Route 110, east of the town center.

The prime interest in this very large cemetery is the grave of John Greenleaf Whittier (1807–92). It lies, very simply marked, within the Whittier family plot. This plot is entirely surrounded by a hedge, and its position is indicated by a sign-post toward the eastern end of the cemetery. Whittier was born down the road in the direction of Haverhill, and he spent fifty-six years of his life in Amesbury. Although everyone has some acquaintance with his poems (including "Snow-Bound" and "Barbara Frietchie"), it is less well remembered that Whittier was an early and vehement abolitionist. He also composed the verses to a large number of hymns, of which the best known is perhaps "Dear Lord and Father of Mankind."

AMHERST

West Cemetery. [89]   Entrance on Triangle Street, a short distance north of the town center.

There is an old section at the back of the cemetery, containing a varied assortment of eighteenth-century stones. But the chief attraction for most visitors is a family plot within the newer section, behind an iron fence. Here is the grave of Emily Dickinson, born 1830, "called back" 1886.

> . . . Since then 'tis centuries, but each
> Feels shorter than the day
> I first surmised the horses' heads
> Were toward eternity.

ARLINGTON

Ancient Burying Ground. [90] At the rear of the Unitarian Church on Pleasant Street (Route 60).

Toward the back of this old cemetery a monument marks the common grave of twelve Revolutionary soldiers who died here on their retreat from Concord and Lexington, April 19, 1775. Elsewhere are interesting slates dating from the 1730's.

BARNSTABLE

Cobb's Hill Cemetery. [91] Behind and to the west of the Unitarian Church, on Route 6A.

Neither as old nor, perhaps, as interesting as the Lothrop Cemetery down the road. Nevertheless this cemetery comprises an attractive combination of periods arranged here and there on a grassy knoll, and it invites a stroll around. The Unitarian churchyard is adjacent.

Lothrop Cemetery. [92] On the south side of Route 6A, between the villages of Barnstable and West Barnstable.

The old section of this attractive cemetery, nearest the road, dates from the seventeenth century; further back is an area currently in use. Most of the older stones are badly worn, but there are several striking exceptions. A number of the most interesting stones mark graves of the Hinckley family. The first of these is the handsome table-stone monument to Thomas Hinckley (d. 1706, ae. 85), a Governor of Plymouth Colony in the seventeenth century. Along the driveway on the western edge of the cemetery is a slate stone of modest size, decorated with a sailing ship: it is "In Memory of Mr. Lot C.

Hinckley," d. 1835, ae. 22. And elsewhere is a marble stone for Mr. Ezra Hinckley, who died in 1849 at Fort Kearney, Pawnee Indian Territory, ae. 33.

The two oldest legible stones are dated 1683. One of these, next to the Thomas Hinckley monument, is in excellent condition. It marks the grave of Dorothy Rawson (d. 1683, ae. 2) ; it is decorated with the classic assortment of fertility emblems in the vegetable mode.

BARRE

Buckminster Cemetery. [93]   On South Street, ¾ mile south of the common.

A well-kept cemetery behind a neat stone wall; several stones bear carving of unusual interest. Slightly to the right of the center, notice the very handsome stones of Coomer Soule (d. 1777) and Sussana Soule (d. 1771), the latter with a long epitaph. Elsewhere, the stones of Captain Josiah Holden and his wife, obviously by the same carver, bear identical, abstract portraits: notice the hair in Medusa-like ringlets.

Lincoln Cemetery. [94]   On Pleasant Street, ⅔ mile north of Route 32.

Under the oak trees at the north end of this attractive cemetery is an interesting monument in marble to Deacon Joshua Rogers (d. 1850). The carving in high relief shows a table covered with a cloth, two goblets, and what appears to be a coffee pot.

BEVERLY

Ancient Burying Ground. [95]   Occupies both sides of Abbott Street behind the First Baptist Church in the center of town.

Several of the most interesting items among the old stones here will be found within the separate Hale family plot, set off by its own stone wall. Not far away notice the fine stone of Mr. Isaac Spofford, "Practitioner in Physic and Surgery," (d. 1786). It features a pointing hand, elaborate carving, and an apt Vergilian epitaph.

Privateer Cemetery. [96]   Along Route 62 (Dane Street), between Hale and Butman Streets.

A large cemetery, attractively wooded. Most of it is relatively modern and of only ordinary interest. Some of the older stones are worth examination, however; in particular a pair of large slate stones standing near the corner of Dane and Butman Streets. These mark the graves of Nancy and Eleanor, two successive wives of Joseph Emerson. Nancy died ae. 25 within eight months of her marriage; Eleanor was married thirteen months later and died within three years. The stones bear graceful and touching epitaphs.

BLANDFORD

Old Burying Ground. [97] On Route 23, in the center of Blandford village.

A small cemetery, very handsome and well kept; it is enclosed by a stone wall and interspersed with tall pine trees. There is a rich collection of fine stones in slate, red sandstone, and marble, dating from the late eighteenth-century. Among numerous interesting examples note the large, elaborate, and curiously shaped slates at the graves of the Reverend Morton and his wife.

BOSTON

Central Burying Ground. [98] At the southeast corner of Boston Common, near Boylston Street. Open 9 A.M.–4 P.M. weekdays.

The Central Burying Ground was established in 1756 to remedy the shortage of burial space in the King's Chapel and Granary burying grounds. This cemetery was originally called "South Burying Ground," when its position lay in fact in the South End of Boston; it was later called "Common Burying Ground" after its location in the Common, and finally "Central" after 1810 when a new "South Burying Ground" was established on Washington Street. The painter Gilbert Stuart (1755–1828) is buried here.

During the construction of the Boston subway in 1895, excavations turned up the remains of an estimated eleven hundred adults in the area of Central Burying Ground. A large slate slab in the northwest corner of the cemetery marks the site of their reinterment.

BARRE

Copp's Hill Burying Ground. [99]   Hull Street, ½ block west of Old North Church. Open 8 A.M.–4 P.M. weekdays.

Established in 1660; occupies a hill overlooking Charlestown to the north, where Paul Revere waited for the signal lights displayed from Old North Church. Later in the Revolutionary War the British used the cemetery for an artillery post from which to shell Charlestown and Bunker Hill.

The Mather tomb within the cemetery marks the graves of Doctors Increase, Cotton, and Samuel Mather, d. 1723, 1727, and 1785, respectively.

Visitors to Copp's Hill should on no account miss the opportunity to visit Old North Church, which is nearby.

Forest Hills Cemetery. [100]   Forest Hills Avenue, off Morton Street (Route 203) in Jamaica Plain. Open 7 A.M. until sunset.

For a large and elaborate nineteenth-century "garden cemetery," Forest Hills is surprisingly little known: this is doubtless the result of its operating, over the years, in the shadow of the even grander Mount Auburn Cemetery in Cambridge. If these two great cemeteries are compared, Forest Hills is inevitably the less imposing. But to admirers of the genre it is unquestionably worth a visit.

The cemetery office (by the entrance gate) will provide a pictorial brochure and a plan of the cemetery listing some of the notable graves. Among those buried here are Edward Everett Hale, William Lloyd Garrison, Eugene O'Neill, and E. E. Cummings.

The cemetery grounds are extensive (260 acres) and fully landscaped, centering on a lake. The more elaborate monuments show an unusually large proportion of standing sculptured females. Individual monuments worth looking for include a bronze relief by Daniel Chester French entitled "Death Staying the Hand of the Sculptor" on the Milmore Memorial, just to the left of the entrance; a bronze eagle, very fierce and fine; and an abstract sculpture resembling an *art nouveau* mushroom. In the far southwest corner, at the intersection of Citron and Laburnum Avenues, is a marble sculpture of a boy sitting with his toys in a small boat: the little figure is dressed in aristocratic nineteenth-century fashion, wearing long curls and skirts instead of trousers. The whole work is encased in a glass box, in the manner of some monuments at Père Lachaise in Paris. The inscription on the front of the base reads, "Mon Fils Bien-Aimé / Louis Ernest Mieusset / Agé de / 4 Ans 9 Mois 6 Jours." Around to one side of the base is the legend in plain English: "Copyright 1889 by Marie Louise Mieusset."

Granary Burying Ground. [101]   Tremont Street, south of Beacon Street. Open 8 A.M.–4 P.M. daily.

The Granary Burying Ground, established 1660, contains the graves of more famous colonial and Revolutionary figures than any other cemetery in Boston. The visitor looking for famous graves may also observe many fine examples of stone-carving on the black slate markers.

Notable people buried here include three signers of the Declaration of Independence, John Hancock, Samuel Adams, and Robert Treat Paine; Peter Faneuil, James Otis, and Paul Revere; the parents of Benjamin Franklin; and the victims of the Boston Massacre of 1770. A group of French protestants who had sought refuge in Boston after the revocation of the Edict of Nantes in 1685 are buried southwest of the Franklin memorial.

In a special category is the grave, not far from that of Paul Revere, of "Mary Goose wife to Isaac Goose . . . Dec^d

October the 9th 1690." This Mary Goose has been thought by many to be the original "Mother Goose" and the compiler, or at least the inspiration, of the famous collection of nursery rhymes. The weight of cold scholarship, however, seems to indicate that the "Mother Goose" tradition began with a French collection, *Contes de ma mère l'oye,* published in 1697.

One of the most handsome gravestones is that of Jabez Smith Jr., "Lieutenant of Marines on board the Continental Ship Trumbull," who has a superb three-masted ship carved at the top of his stone where others have skulls and wings.

King's Chapel Burying Ground. [102] Tremont Street, north of Beacon Street. Open 8 A.M.–4 P.M. daily.

Established 1630, the oldest cemetery in Boston. Contains a fine collection of slate stones from the seventeenth and eighteenth centuries, bearing a wide range of typical ornamentations; particularly noteworthy are two stones near the entrance depicting a struggle between the figures of Time and Death.

Notable people buried here include a long list of governors of Massachusetts and of Connecticut, among them Governor John Winthrop (1588–1649).

To the left of the Chapel itself is a large obelisk, a memorial to the Chevalier de Saint Sauveur, a French naval officer who aided the United States during the Revolution. The monument (erected in a flush of Franco-American amity in 1916) bears a lengthy and elegant epitaph in French: among several interesting features the epitaph contains a hearty curse upon any who may in the future attempt to sever the bonds of friendship joining France and America.

Phipps Street Burying Grounds. [103] Charlestown, at the end of Phipps Street: this is four blocks north along Main Street from the Thompson Square station of the MBTA, then one block west.

Unfortunately, this important cemetery is kept locked. It can be opened by arrangement with the Cemetery Division of the Boston Parks Department: telephone (617) 298-8750.

At Phipps Street is a neatly trimmed oasis of seventeenth-century Boston, surrounded by a near-desert of urban renewal and elevated highways. Many of the graves are marked by excellent examples of early stonecutting: note among others the stone of Elizabeth Codman (d. 1708), with its elaborate vegetable/fertility emblems.

The most conspicuous monument is that erected to John Harvard in 1828. Harvard emigrated from England to Charlestown in 1637, serving as assistant pastor of the First Church; he died the very next year, leaving half his estate (£780) and his small library to a newly-founded educational institution in Cambridge, Mass.

BOXFORD

"The Cemetery by the Nursery." [104] On Ipswich Road, ⅓ mile west of the turn-off from the Boxford-Rowley Road.

This small, out-of-the-way cemetery, of which the name seems to have been forgotten, is worth finding for the sake of one remarkable monument. In one corner, by the road, is the tomb of General Solomon Low (d. 1861) and his four wives. The General is represented by a handsome medallion in the center. To the left is a marble tablet with the names of the two wives who bore him children, Huldah and Dolly: they are shown holding bouncing babes at the breast. To the right, a second tablet bears the names of two childless wives, Martha and Caroline. These good women are shown reading their Bibles.

There is an interesting monument in the first row to the Hon. Aaron Wood, who "suddenly expired" in 1791, leaving a valuable estate "toward supporting a Grammar School, forever, in the town of Boxford, his native place."

BRIMFIELD

Brimfield Cemetery. [105]   On Route 19, just south of Route 20.

The old section of this large town cemetery is worth a brief visit for those in the vicinity. At the far north end, the best example among several similar stones, is an extraordinarily handsome white marble stone marking "Capt. Aaron Charles'is Grave." It features a very beautiful vine-like pattern of hearts. Not far away is the granite marker of Mr. John Bliss, who "died June 28th 1804, by a hurt from a plow, in the 29th year of his age."

BURLINGTON

Old Burying Ground. [106]   On Bedford Street, just west of the village green, across from Simonds Park.

Burlington had its origin as the second parish of the town of Woburn: its burying ground was established in 1730. Notice the handsome portrait stone of the Rev. Mr. Thomas Jones (d. 1774) and, next to it, the much more modest stone of the Rev. Mr. Supply Clap (d. 1747), his predecessor at the Second Church of Christ in Woburn.

BOSTON

Near to these is an interesting, highly patriotic stone for Charles Pratt Marston, who died in 1777 aged nine months, "While British Forces held his native Town." The epitaph concludes:

Then shalt thou rise, where dwells Immortal Love
And with great CAMDEN live in brightest Realms above.

Lord Camden a great friend of America & after whom the Child was named.

Charles Pratt, Lord Camden (1714–94), was an English lord chancellor noted for his defense of the American colonists in the House of Lords.

CAMBRIDGE

Mount Auburn Cemetery. [107] Mount Auburn Street. Open daily 8 A.M.–7 P.M. (summer), 8 A.M.–5 P.M. (winter).

Mount Auburn was established in 1831 as the first "garden cemetery" in America. Behind its Egyptian Gates are 170 acres of landscaped grounds comprising an extremely attractive park: since each tree of the highly diverse collection is labelled, the Cemetery also makes a fine arboretum. The monuments include many examples of the splendid and extravagant nineteenth-century style. The visitor with a taste for such mortuary grandeur could easily spend an entire day here.

Certain of the most famous monuments should on no account be missed. These include the memorial to Mary Baker Eddy (1821–1910), in a commanding position overlooking "Halcyon Lake"; the massive Sphinx, a memorial to the preservation of the Union, bearing the motto "America Conservata / Africa Liberata"; and the Slave Monument, a memorial to

Charles Torrey, a Boston abolitionist who was caught helping fugitive slaves to escape and who died in a Maryland prison. Two splendid examples of the high style in epitaphs are to be found on the obelisks of two brothers named Fuller: these stand just to the east of the tower in the center of the cemetery. Light relief to these imposing monuments may be had by looking for the statues of dogs at Mount Auburn. There are at least four of them.

Famous people buried at Mount Auburn make a very long list indeed. Among them are Louis Agassiz, Thomas B. Aldrich, Charles Bulfinch, William Ellery Channing, Dorothy Dix, Charles Dana Gibson, Oliver Wendell Holmes, Julia Ward Howe, Henry Wadsworth Longfellow, Amy Lowell, Charles Eliot Norton, Francis Parkman, Josiah Quincy, Charles Sumner, and Theodore Thomas.

Plans of the cemetery, containing a key to the location of noted graves and monuments, are available at the office by the front entrance. The Cemetery also publishes a book containing biographies of noted people buried within.

Birdwatchers may obtain from the office, for a fee of 75¢, keys enabling them to enter the cemetery grounds at dawn.

Old Town Burying Ground. [108] Between Christ Church and First Parish Church on Garden Street, near Harvard Square.

The old cemetery in Cambridge dates from 1636, the year Harvard College received its charter. In it are buried most of the early inhabitants of the town and several of the first Harvard presidents. There are numerous seventeenth-century stones in good condition, some decorated with elaborate symbolism: one superb example is the stone of Capt. Jonathan Remington (d. 1700), near the brick walkway in the center of the yard. A number of Latin inscriptions will provide diversion for some visitors.

CHELMSFORD

Forefathers' Burying Ground. [109]   In the center of Chelmsford village, behind the First Parish Unitarian-Universalist Church.

A handsome cemetery, an attractive setting, a large number of old and interesting stones. The earliest legible inscription is dated 1690. There are forty-seven Revolutionary soldiers buried here; a monument to their memory stands nearby on the Common.

One of the saddest of the old stones marks the multiple grave of the wife and four children of Lt. Benjamin Fletcher, all of whom died between September 24 and October 5, 1778. The most elaborate stonecutting can be seen on the large adjacent slates of Col. Jonas Clark and his wife Elizabeth, near the center of the old section.

CONCORD

Hillside Burying Ground. [110]   On the north side of the town square.

The old burying ground in Concord enjoys one of the most attractive settings of all early New England cemeteries. The site is historic in itself: on the crest of the hill was Concord's first meeting house as well as the town's "Liberty Pole" during the Revolution. There are graves of numerous Revolutionary War heroes: among them, the fine monument and epitaph to

Col. John Buttrick, who commanded the militia in the first attack on British troops at Concord North Bridge on April 19, 1775.

Two of the most interesting stones mark the graves of lesser-known persons. The marble stone on the hillside, not far from the entrance, was, it is said, the first white stone among the many slate ones and accordingly quite a novelty. It bears the inscription, "designed by its durability to perpetuate the memory and by its colour to signify the moral character of Miss Abigail Dudley who died here June 4, 1812, aged 73." The most famous of all stones here is easily found by proceeding straight ahead over the crest of the hill and a few steps down the other side. Here a slate stone marks the grave of a former slave who had bought his freedom: "John Jack a native of Africa, who died March 1773 aged about sixty years. Tho' born in a land of slavery, he was born free. Though he lived in a land of liberty, he lived a slave. . . ."

Sleepy Hollow Cemetery. [111]   On Court Lane, just north of the town square.

The second of Concord's two famous cemeteries, established in the mid-nineteenth century, is noteworthy for its very extensive, wooded grounds, and for a small area known as "Authors' Ridge" which contains the graves of several of New England's greatest literary figures.

"Authors' Ridge" is most easily found from the main gate of the cemetery. From here small markers indicate the way to a path, with hand-railing, that leads uphill to the authors' graves. The signs marking the way are cut, very decorously, to resemble gravestones—which may make them somewhat difficult to distinguish.

Following the path to the top of the small ridge the visitor will find, close together, the burial plots of the Thoreau, Hawthorne, and Alcott families. Several yards further on is the much larger Emerson family plot. Ralph Waldo Emerson's gravestone is a huge uncut granite boulder bearing a plaque. The way to the tomb of the sculptor Daniel Chester French (1850–1931) is also marked with gravestone-signs.

Among other notable people buried here is Ephraim Bull, who developed the Concord grape but failed to profit financially from his work: his stone bears the epitaph, "He sowed, others reaped."

 South Burying Place. [112] In the village center, next to the savings bank.

Overshadowed by Concord's two more famous cemeteries, the South Burying Place is nevertheless in some respects the most interesting of the three. As the burying ground for some of the wealthiest families of eighteenth-century Concord, it not surprisingly contains an outstanding collection of slate stones from the finest and most elaborate period of New England stonecutting. Visitors whose primary interest is the complex and beautiful designs obtainable in slate where expense was no object will count this small graveyard among their favorites.

One stone in particular would attract immediate attention even without mention here: it is the huge, thick, magnificently carved slate stone of John Lee (d. 1671). A group of particularly fine stones marks the graves of the Jones family at the rear of the cemetery. But the general standard here is very high indeed, and many of the less imposing stones of this yard would make prize items elsewhere.

BREWSTER

DANVERS

Nurse Family Graveyard. [113]   At the intersection of Pine and Adams Streets is a driveway leading across the fields to the Nurse House (may be visited). Follow this same driveway in past the house and continue another 150 yards to the graveyard.

The handsome, austere Nurse House, in classic saltbox style, was erected in 1678: this small plot behind it was chosen as the family graveyard. Only modern monuments remain today. Of interest is a large monument erected in 1885 to Rebecca Nurse, "In loving memory of her Christian character."

Rebecca, the wife of Francis Nurse, has left behind her the reputation of a near-saintly goodness. Still she was accused of witchcraft in April, 1692 and subsequently executed, although her neighbors testified to her innocence. The inscription reads, "Accused of Witchcraft She declared, 'I am innocent and God will clear my innocency.' Once acquitted yet falsely condemned She suffered death July 19, 1692." There is an epitaph composed by John Greenleaf Whittier.

> O Christian martyr who for Truth could die
> When all about thee owned the hideous lie!
> The world redeemed from Superstition's sway
> Is breathing freer for thy sake to-day.

Another granite monument lists the names of those who testified to Rebecca's innocence.

Wadsworth Burial Ground. [114]   On Summer Street, just north of Maple Street (Route 62).

Danvers began as Salem Village, an outlying colony of the Town of Salem; it did not become a separate township until 1757. The early settlers of Salem Village were buried here, beginning in the 1640's. Most of the old graves are no longer marked. Two of the most interesting stones, as is often the case, mark the graves of local pastors. There is a very handsome marker for the Rev. Mr. Peter Clark, "the painfull Labourious & faithfull Pastor of the first Church in this Town," (d. 1768). The stone of the Rev. Dr. Joseph Green (d. 1719) is something of a rarity for New England, being written entirely in Latin.

The greatest historical interest attaches to the small stone, toward the back, of Elizabeth Parris (d. 1696). It was in the house of her father, the Rev. Samuel Parris, that the Salem witch mania began in 1692—and Elizabeth was involved at the very beginning.

The most notable episode of mass hysteria in American history, culminating in the infamous Salem witch trials, had its origin in the parish of Salem which is today the town of Danvers. More precisely, the witch craze appears to have begun by the fireside of the parsonage occupied by the Rev. Samuel Parris. His daughter and niece, Elizabeth Parris and Abigail Williams, would sit there to listen to moving stories of witchcraft and voodoo told by Tituba, the family slave. It was the dark winter of 1692, and the woods beyond the small settlement were full of demons. The girls became hysterical, and soon communicated their derangement to the other adolescent girls of Salem Village. Seeing their daughters screaming, jumping around, and falling into fits, the pious citizens were ready enough to believe the diagnosis of the village doctor: that the girls were victims of witchcraft. Pressed to say who had bewitched them, the girls named three women of the village—Tituba being one of them. When the three women were examined by magistrates, the girls went into fits on the floor of the courtroom; finally Tituba admitted that she had been riding a broomstick and conversing with the devil. The women were then put in jail.

The worst was yet to come. Other women of Salem decided that their various ailments were caused by the witchcraft of their neighbors; accusations multiplied; by April, hundreds of men and women had been summarily examined and jailed. The witchcraft court, composed of distinguished judges, was convened in Salem in June. It set to its work with dispatch: by September, twenty people had been executed and at least three more had died in prison awaiting trial. Then, curiously, the frenzy abated as quickly as it had arisen. By January, 1693, those persons still in prison were acquitted. People had lost interest.

The most famous of the witchcraft judges was Samuel Sewall, later Chief Justice of the Massachusetts Colony. Sewall was the only member of the witchcraft court to acknowledge later the wrong that had been done. In 1697, at Old South Church, Boston, Sewall publicly declared the error of the proceedings and accepted the "blame and shame" for his part in it. Each year thereafter he spent a day in fasting and repentance.

DEDHAM

Old Parish Burying Ground. [115] On Village Avenue, near the town center.

The old cemetery at Dedham was established near the middle of the seventeenth century: the oldest legible stone is dated 1678. Historical interest centers on one tomb, marked as the final resting place of Timothy Dwight, d. 1718 ae. 88; an inscription has been added, celebrating Captain Timothy as "The Ancestor Of the Dwight family in America: A Family like himself, Trusty, serious and Godly. . . ." Interestingly enough, Dwight does not lie in a tomb of his own; rather, he and his wife Bethiah, who died a week after he did, were placed in a tomb which already contained the bodies of two Dedham notables, Major Elezar Lusher and the Reverend

William Adams. The ceremony is described in an interesting passage from the diaries of Samuel Sewall, a distinguished justice (who, incidentally, took part in the Salem witchcraft trials) :

> Friday, February 7, 1717–8:—Col. Townsend, Sam¹ Lynde esqr and I go in the Hackney Coach to Dedham to the Funeral of Capt. Dwight and his wife. Govʳ Dudley went in his Chariot. Din'd at Mr. Belcher's by his Direction, and the Coffin brought and set down at his Gate: Bearers thence, Govʳ Dudley and Sewall; Townsend, Lynde; Nathan¹ Hubbard esqr., Kingsbury. Bearers of the woman I know not: were put in Major Lusher's Tomb. Came from Mr. Belcher's when the Sun was hardly an hour high. Got home comfortably before 8. *Laus Deo*. It seems Mr. Adams lyes in this Tomb into which I have now again looked. Lord mercifully fit me for the time of my Dissolution.

Pine Ridge Cemetery. [116]   Reached by a driveway leading uphill at 238 Pine Street. Open daily, 10 A.M.–5 P.M.

The Pine Ridge Cemetery for Small Animals, established in 1907, is operated by the Animal Rescue League of Boston. It has a pleasantly wooded hillside setting. The most famous animal buried here is undoubtedly Admiral Byrd's dog, Igloo: he is buried beneath a granite iceberg bearing the inscription, "More than a Friend." Other interesting memorials include a stone inscribed, "To the many dogs who have given their lives in service to man," and, at one grave, the figure of a small dog poking its head out of a briefcase—evidently a favorite trick. It is to be noted that a large proportion of the stones bear some kind of epitaph; several have cameo photographs of the deceased, a familiar practice in Italian cemeteries but most unusual in New England.

DEERFIELD

Old Burying Ground. [117]   In Old Deerfield on Albany Road, which runs westward from Old Deerfield Street through Deerfield Academy.

The Burying Ground of Old Deerfield is justly famous for its beauty, its flawless preservation, and its interesting stones. The restored village of Old Deerfield provides the perfect setting.

Specific historical interest centers on the grassy mound in the southeast corner. This is the common grave of the forty-eight victims of the Deerfield Massacre of February 29, 1704. Most of the remaining inhabitants were taken as captives to Canada, and many were killed on the way.

The general standard of the stones here is very high. The earliest examples date from the late seventeenth century. One unusual stone stands under the trees near the center of the graveyard: this is the marker of Mrs. Abigail Williams (d. 1754), using for its central emblem a large and handsome clock face. The most agreeable epitaph appears on the stone of Lt. Mehuman Hinsdell, d. 1736 ae. 63, who "was the first male child born in this place and was twice captivated by the Indian salvages."

DUXBURY

Miles Standish Burying Ground. [118]   On Chestnut Street, which runs southwest from the "five corners" intersection at South Duxbury.

A very handsome and well-kept cemetery, at the site of the town's first meeting house: it was in use from 1637–1787. The oldest legible stone, of the Rev. Ichabod Wiswall, is dated 1700. Here are buried Miles Standish, Jonathan Alden, and, it

Persecuted for
wearing the beard.

LEOMINSTER

is thought, John and Priscilla Alden as well: all the leading characters of Longfellow's poem, "The Courtship of Miles Standish." The presumed location of these graves is carefully marked.

Mayflower Cemetery. [119]   On Route 3A (Tremont Street), next to First Parish Church.

This large, handsomely wooded cemetery was established in 1787; the most interesting stones are in the old section, nearest the church. Several of the old slates have been carefully restored. One of the stones, not far from the church, bears a famous and curious epitaph. It marks the grave of Aseneath Soule, widow of Simeon Soule, d. 1865 ae. 87, and carries the legend, "The Chisel can't help her any."

FALL RIVER

Oak Grove Cemetery. [120]   At the head of Prospect Street, which runs east from Robeson Street.

An extensive, nineteenth-century cemetery, which will please those with a taste for the grand style of monument and for the macabre. The visitor will soon perceive that virtually all the most elaborate monuments were erected by one or another branch of the Borden family. On one side the marble figure of B. H. Borden stands atop a pillar; on another, an elegantly draped female figure towers above a plot of Bordens; here in the center, a handsome Civil War monument bears the inscription, "Erected by Richard Borden." Some distance to the south of these impressive statues is a far more modest plot which holds a deeper fascination. It contains a central slab, again marked with Borden family names, and a number of low headstones. Interest naturally centers on the stones marked "A.J.B.," "A.D.B.," and "Lizbeth."

It was on August 4, 1892, that Lizzie Andrew Borden allegedly took an axe, gave her stepmother forty whacks, and then, seeing what she had done, proceeded to give her father forty-one. Andrew Jackson Borden and Abby Durfee Borden were subsequently buried in Oak Grove Cemetery. Lizzie was tried for the double murder and acquitted. As the family home at 92 Second Street, Fall River, now held unpleasant associations, she and her sister Emma used some of their inheritance to purchase "Maplecroft," a spacious house on fashionable French Street, where Lizzie remained until her death in 1927. She was occasionally seen driving about the town behind a handsome pair of horses; and in keeping with her newly genteel style of life, she took to using a slightly altered name. Thus she lies buried as "Lizbeth Andrews Borden." The family plot is well kept, and properly so. By the first provision of her will, Lizzie Borden left the sum of five hundred dollars to the City of Fall River, "the income to be derived therefrom to be used for the perpetual care of my father's lot in Oak Grove Cemetery in said Fall River."

FALMOUTH

Old Town Burying Ground. [121]   Entrance is by a lane off Mill Road, at the junction of Mill Road and the Falmouth-Woods Hole Road, south of Route 28.

There is not a great deal here to be examined, but the cemetery comprises a large, secluded green where one may agreeably spend a quiet half hour. The graves are at the site of the town's first meeting house and training field. The earliest legible stone is dated 1705; there are many graves of Revolutionary soldiers and some interesting carvings on the old slates.

FOXBORO

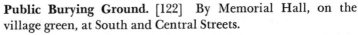

Public Burying Ground. [122] By Memorial Hall, on the village green, at South and Central Streets.

A sign on a tree explains that this small cemetery was given to the town in 1783 by Nehemiah Carpenter, "for that and that only." There are several attractive stones and, in back of Memorial Hall, one extraordinary monument. Attached by a chain to a marble pedestal is a cast-iron object looking like a giant candle-snuffer. Raising this object reveals a circular marble slab beneath, engraved in memory of Mr. Zadok Howe; within the snuffer itself is a second circular slab, engraved with a *memento mori* admonition. The memorial was "erected by Dr. Miller" to his friend Mr. Howe; yet it was, according to an inscription, "wrought by the deceased" in 1810 and repaired by his son in 1841. It would seem that Dr. Miller commissioned his friend Howe, a metalworker, to design a monument for himself. It is a tribute to the civic virtues of Foxboro that this unusual and fragile monument remains both accessible and, although cracked, in relatively good repair.

GRANVILLE

Old Burying Ground. [123] On the north side of Route 57, ¼ mile west of the town hall in Granville Center.

An attractive roadside cemetery on a hillside in wooded surroundings; it contains several stones of particular interest. A short distance from the main entrance, a monument in red sandstone marks the grave of "Mr. Asa Burt who was killed by the Fall of a Tree Jan. 28 AD 1774." Not far away, a white marble stone stands in memory of two ladies: Miss Hannah Bancroft and her friend Mrs. Ruth Strickland, "who died

(Suddenly, while on a visit from Vermont to this Town, the place of her birth) March 2nd 1813. . . ."

HADLEY

Old Hadley Cemetery. [124] On Cemetary Road at the western edge of the village. Cemetary Road is the next street to the north of Route 9, parallel to it.

At the western end of the varied and attractive cemetery is an unusually interesting collection of old stones of various types, in slate, marble, and red sandstone. There is an extraordinarily high proportion of "homemade" stones, better cut than is usually the case, so that they are mostly legible. An elaborate table stone covers the grave of "Reverend Russell's Remains who first gathered and for 35 years faithfully goverened the flock of Christ in Hadley til the cheif shepherd suddenly but mercifully called him off to receive his reward. . . ." Nearby, note the beautiful double headstone in white marble of Capt. Moses and Mrs. Elizabeth Porter.

HARVARD

Old Burial Ground. [125] In the village center, on Route 111.

Not overly picturesque as a whole, the old section of this cemetery nevertheless contains stones of particular interest to students of carving styles. Among the mid-eighteenth-century slates, note the proliferation of an unusual design which is very common here: it features a highly stylized, nearly circular face with geometric decorations. These striking stones, which seem to carry a far more sobering *memento mori* than any

105

skull-and-crossbones, have been identified by Mrs. Forbes and other authorities as the work of Jonathan and Moses Worcester, father and son, who worked in Harvard. Similar examples may be found in neighboring towns.

HAVERHILL

Old Bradford Burying Ground. [126]   In Bradford, the section of Haverhill lying south of the river; opposite the Bradford Tavern on Salem Street. Salem Street runs to the southeast from the green in the center of Bradford.

Small, old, and attractive, containing much that is interesting and one set of stones that is downright scandalous. Standing in a row behind a small obelisk in the middle of the cemetery are seven large slate stones, marking the graves of the Hon. Nathaniel Thurston plus the first six of his seven wives. Thurston's gravestone attests to a distinguished public career; the story of his varied domestic life is told by the other stones, as follows—

Nathaniel Thurston d. 1811, ae. 56

Betsey	d. 1790, ae. 34
Martha	d. 1799, ae. 32
Huldah	d. 1801, ae. 24
Clarrissa	d. 1803, ae. 36
Martha	d. 1804, ae. 25
Mary	d. 1808, ae. 27

The reader will draw his own conclusions, as Thurston's neighbors did at the time. Thurston died in New York State; it is said that his seventh wife rode back to Bradford with the coffin, to see it buried alongside her predecessors. She herself declined to be buried with the rest of the family.

LEXINGTON

IPSWICH

Old Burying Ground. [127]   On High Street, which starts to the east of the village green and runs north.

A large and very attractive cemetery, running up a long slope in a series of terraces. The old section, near the road, was laid out in 1634: there remains a generous and interesting assortment of old stones. The charming view from the top of the hill makes the climb worthwhile.

Among the old monuments note in particular the large portrait stone of the Rev. Nathaniel Rogers (d. 1775), with the portrait much larger than usual; and the stone of John Denison (d. 1747, ae. 25), decorated lavishly with columns and the family coat of arms. An epitaph reads, "His genius, learning, and engaging manners, spoke him the future joy & ornament of his native town. But Heaven meant otherwise. . . ."

LAKEVILLE

Pond Cemetery. [128]   On the shore of Assawompsett Pond; 1¼ miles south of village on Route 18.

Of minor interest historically, but pleasantly situated and worth a stop. The cemetery has been in continuous use since the eighteenth century; some good stones remain. Many Indians are buried here but their graves, as usual, are unmarked.

LANESBORO

Center Cemetery. [129]   On Route 7 (Main Street), opposite St. Luke's Church.

There are several stones here from the late eighteenth century; they are not as easy to spot as is usually the case, since they are cut of the same soft white marble as the stones of the nineteenth century. Some show an interesting, stylized head-and-wings pattern; others bear very handsome calligraphy with no illustration, which is somewhat unusual for the period.

Two graves of noted persons are easily found. One is a table-stone monument to Jonathan Smith, "whose speech in support of the Constitution carried the day for Massachusetts." The other, a large piece of granite, fenced-off and further back, is the grave of Josh Billings.

"Josh Billings" was the intentionally rural-sounding pseudonym of Henry Wheeler Shaw (1818–85), a Lanesboro man whose hayseed humor made him as famous in the nineteenth century as his contemporaries Mark Twain and Bret Harte. Born to a family accustomed to public life, Billings left Lanesboro at an early age and traveled west, becoming a farmer and an auctioneer. In 1860 he began to publish his rural-dialect sketches and soon became a popular lecturer as well. Our great-grandfathers enjoyed this sort of thing:

Qu.—How fast duz sound travel?

Ans.—This depends a good deal upon the natur ov the noize yu are talking about. The sound ov a dinner horn, for instance, travels a half a mile in a seckoned, while an invitashun tew git up in morning I hav known to be 3 quarters ov an hour going up two pair ov stairs, and then not have strength enuff left tew be heard.

Woman iz the glass ware ov kreashun. She iz luvly, and brittle, but she hez run up everything we really enjoy in this life from 25 cents on the dollar to par. Adam, without Eve, would hav been az stupid a game az playing checkures alone. . . .

LENOX

Church on the Hill Cemetery. [130] At Main and Greenwood Streets.

The most attractive feature of this Lenox graveyard is undoubtedly its charming hillside setting, at the side of a handsome white church, overlooking the village. The oldest and most interesting stones are near the church: these include the graves of Jonathan Hinsdale, who about 1750 became the first settler in Lenox, and of Major General John Paterson of the Revolutionary War. Several of the stones nearby are interesting examples of local stonecutting, e.g., the stone of "Thankfull wife of Elias Willard," d. 1789.

LEOMINSTER

Evergreen Cemetery. [131] On North Main Street (route 13), just south of route 2.

There is only one reason to visit Evergreen Cemetery, but it is one good reason. In the first row of graves by the road, slightly south of the main gate, is the memorial to Joseph Palmer, d. October 30, 1873: the marble monument bears a relief carving of Palmer's head wearing a full, spade-shaped beard, and the motto "Persecuted for wearing the beard."

The greatest surprise in the odd story of Joseph Palmer is the realization that the familiar stereotype of the dignified, bearded Americans of the nineteenth century is valid only from the 1850's on. Lincoln wore his famous beard only after his inauguration in 1860, and the earliest representation of a bearded Uncle Sam dates from 1858. In the 1830's beards were downright rare; and when Joseph Palmer, living between Leominster and Fitchburg, decided to grow one, his neighbors did not regard his eccentricity with tolerance. Palmer was taunted as "Old Jew Palmer" (it was assumed in 1830 that only Jews wore beards); he was denounced from the local pulpits; once in Fitchburg he was set upon by four men, armed with soap and a razor, who intended to shave him by force. After the struggle that followed, Palmer was thrown into jail, charged with causing an affray. He refused to pay a small fine and remained in jail much longer than he might otherwise have had to.

This rather prickly character later joined Fruitlands, the utopian community founded by Bronson Alcott at Harvard, Massachusetts. When Fruitlands failed (after only six months), Palmer stayed on, renamed the place Freelands, and operated it as a hostel for tramps and wayfarers. He remained at Freelands until his death. The fine bearded monument would doubtless have pleased him.

LEXINGTON

Old Burying Ground. [132]   Entrance is by a path to the west of the First Parish Church, on Lexington Green.

An important historic cemetery that is also exceptionally attractive. Lexington's part in the Revolution is marked by the memorial to Captain Parker, who led the militia company that fired the first American shots of the war, on Lexington Green, April 19, 1775. On the Green itself is another monument, recording the words (perhaps apocryphal) of Captain Parker's

command: "Stand your ground. Don't fire unless fired upon. But if they mean to have a war let it begin here."

Besides the graves of Revolutionary soldiers there are numerous stones of considerable interest; at one end of the cemetery they stand arranged in a curious semicircular pattern. Note among others the large slate stone above the grave of the six children of Abijah and Sarah Childs, all of whom died between August 19 and September 6, 1778.

L O W E L L

Lowell Cemetery. [133]   At 1020 Lawrence Street, near the southern edge of the city. There is easy access to Lawrence Street from Route 495 at the exit marked "Woburn Street / South Lowell."

A large, Victorian cemetery which will please those with a taste for the grand style in monuments. One item of interest is a ponderous Egyptian mausoleum erected in memory of Eli Hoyt Shedd, d. 1885 ae. 8. Another mausoleum is a miniature church in brownstone, a memorial to a Dr. Parker. Everywhere are broken urns, sheaves, tree stumps, angels; here an armchair, there a headless dog. What is genuinely magnificent is a beautiful lion, his head resting sorrowfully on his paws. This most striking monument bears no name.

M A N C H E S T E R

Old Burying Ground. [134]   On Route 127 (Washington Street).

Small and very picturesque, set with many tall and beautiful pine trees. The burying ground dates from 1661, though the

112

LOWELL

earliest legible stones are from the mid-eighteenth century. Notice, near the southwest corner, the stone of Col. Benjamin Marston (d. 1754), with a fierce skull-and-crossbones; and near to it, the small stone of Philomela Parish (d. 1793, ae. 13 days), bearing a faint but very fine sunburst design.

MARBLEHEAD

Old Burial Hill. [135]   On Orne Street, by Redd's Pond.

Burial Hill at Marblehead combines a beautiful setting, numerous exceptional carvings, and a high proportion of epitaphs: the whole invites a lengthy visit. The graves are spread over a hill, the site of the first meeting house in 1638; from the top there is a charming view of the harbor. An estimated six hundred Revolutionary soldiers are buried here.

Two stones which should not be missed stand side by side near the crest of the hill, the original slate now encased in granite. They mark the graves of the Rev. William Whitwell (d. 1781) and Anna Barnard (d. 1774), both decorated with remarkable portrait engravings. Nearby is an obelisk monument to sixty-five fishermen, lost "on the Grand Banks of Newfoundland in the memorable gale of Sept. 19, 1846." Ten Marblehead ships were lost in the gale. Also on the top of the hill is another elaborate slate, now in a protective casing: the famous stone of Mrs. Susanna Jayne, d. 1776. This extraordinarily eclectic design includes an hourglass, bones, angels, and bats; the central figure is a skeleton, with a scythe and a laurel wreath, holding in his hands the sun and the moon; he is surrounded by a snake eating its tail. One wonders whether this marvellous and complex imagery finally represented a conception of death any more profound than that of a poor man whose monument to his wife was a simple fieldstone.

M A R L B O R O U G H

Spring Hill Cemetery. [136]   The entrance is off High Street. High Street begins near the Congregational Church, running above Route 20 and parallel to it.

The old stones in this semi-abandoned cemetery share in the generally high quality of eighteenth-century work in this area. Two distinctive styles are well represented. One features what might be called "individualized" angels or cherubim—a graceful compromise between the portrait stone and the traditional winged figure. An especially fine example here is the stone of Deacon Andrew Rice. Also in evidence is the unusual geometric style associated with the stonecutters of Harvard, Massachusetts.

M A R S H F I E L D

Winslow Burying Ground. [137]   The road to the cemetery leads off Webster Street, about two miles south of the village center and Route 139. The junction of Webster Street and Winslow Cemetery Road is indicated by a historical marker.

Until recently, this small cemetery containing the grave of Daniel Webster was distinctly isolated, requiring a walk across country from Webster Street. It is now a modest anomaly amid the usual suburban development. Nevertheless it is appropriate, in a way, for the old burying ground to be surrounded by citizens of Marshfield, for such was certainly the original intention. The knoll on which it stands was the site of the town's first meeting house in 1641; as was customary, the burying ground was established not out at the edge of town but right in the center of things. Subsequent patterns of settlement which left the graveyard to one side have now brought it back into the fold.

The Webster monument is naturally the main attraction. Still, the name of the cemetery reflects a long-standing prior claim to local distinction, that of Josiah Winslow (d. 1680), a Governor of New Plymouth Colony. Winslow was born in Plymouth and was the first American-born governor of an American colony. The Webster and Winslow family plots are set off by iron railings. Other stones date back to the early eighteenth century. Many are broken, but many are clearly legible, with fine carvings and epitaphs.

Winslow Burying Ground is the scene of the memorable opening of Stephen Vincent Benét's "The Devil and Daniel Webster."

Yes, Dan'l Webster's dead—or, at least, they buried him. But every time there's a thunder storm around Marshfield, they say you can hear his rolling voice in the hollows of the sky. And they say that if you go to his grave and speak loud and clear, "Dan'l Webster—Dan'l Webster!" the ground'll begin to shiver and the trees begin to shake. And after a while you'll hear a deep voice saying, "Neighbor, how stands the Union?" Then you better answer the Union stands as she stood, rock-bottomed and copper-sheathed, one and indivisible, or he's liable to rear right out of the ground. At least, that's what I was told when I was a youngster.

MARTHA'S VINEYARD

Edgartown Cemetery. [138] On Pease Point Way between Cooke Street and Robinson Road.

A large, attractive cemetery, particularly well kept, enhanced by many varieties of trees and shrubs. The oldest stones date from the 1780's and are generally in good condition. Epitaphs of sea captains and others who died at sea provide a reminder of the days when the Vineyard's industry dealt in whales, not tourists.

MIDDLEBORO

Church on the Green Cemetery. [139]   On East Main Street (Route 105), just west of the junction, with Route 44; opposite the First Congregational Church.

The cemetery contains a large number of old slates of more than usual interest. Note the stones, side by side toward the northwest corner, of "that truly Evangelic Preacher, that amiable Pattern of Charity in all its Branches, the Rev. Silvanus Conant"—pastor of the church opposite—and of his wife Abigail. Among these old stones of modest proportions stands a huge obelisk of polished black granite. It is a remarkable piece of work, remarkably out of place here.

MILTON

Milton Cemetery. [140]   On Centre Street, east of Randolph Avenue.

Of interest here is the old section, near the road, of a large, modern cemetery. In such a setting old gravestones have the undeniable benefit of careful maintenance; though it must be admitted that they lose some of the charm they would retain, even when overgrown, in a smaller cemetery exclusively of the period. Still, some of the old slates here are particularly fine. Note among others the portrait stone of Mrs. Mary Vose (d. 1792) and her three children.

117

In a more recent section of the cemetery is the grave of Wendell Phillips (1811–84), the distinguished orator and radical abolitionist. The cause of Abolition attracted men who held what were, for the time, extremist political views: Phillips attacked Lincoln for his moderation on the emancipation question and later advocated such causes as prohibition and the abolition of capital punishment. And there can have been few Americans in public life who, like Phillips, defended the Paris Commune of 1871.

NANTUCKET

 Old North Burying Ground. [141]   On New Lane, reached from the center of Nantucket village via Main Street. The "New North" cemetery is opposite.

On the extreme south side of the old cemetery are several of the most interesting monuments. Near the road is a stone describing the career of Robert Ratliff, an English seaman. His first exploit was to take part in the British raid on Washington in 1814; in 1818 he was a member of the escort taking Napoleon to St. Helena; and in 1820 he was shipwrecked on Nantucket, where he remained until his death in 1882. Further back are two adjacent stones bearing identical designs and wording: they mark the graves of Amos Otis and Thomas Delap, both of Barnstable, both "Cast a shore on Nantucket December the 6th 1771 & perish't in the Snowstorm there." And behind these is the grave of Thomas Davis, d. 1763 ae. 19, who "Departed this life at Sea (in the Lat. 38 Deg. N. Long 65 Deg. W.)."

Elsewhere in the cemetery is the grave of Robert Inot, commander of the *Savannah,* the first steamship to cross the Atlantic, sailing from Savannah, Georgia to Liverpool in 1819.

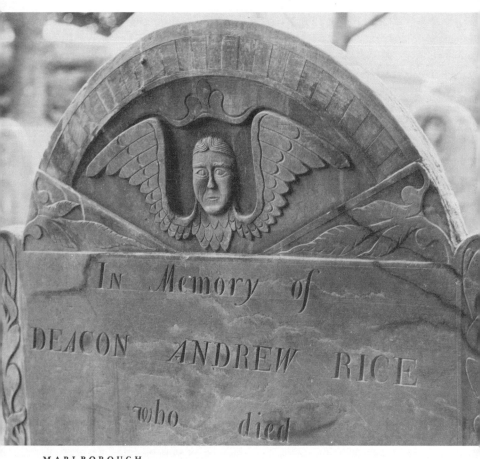

In Memory of

DEACON ANDREW RICE

who died

MARLBOROUGH

NEWBURYPORT

Old Hill Burying Ground. [142]   In the center of the village, lying across Bartlett Mall from High Street.

A large cemetery of mainly eighteenth-century composition: its setting is exceptionally attractive, and there are numerous handsome and interesting stones. From the top of the hill there is a fine view of the beautiful village of Newburyport.

The most famous gravestone in Newburyport is readily found at the top of the hill. This is the large and handsome slate of Mrs. Mary McHard, who ". . . was in a state of health suddenly summoned to the Skies & snatched from the eager embraces of her friends, (and the throbbing hearts of her disconsolate family confessed their fairest prospects of sublunary bliss were in one moment dashed) by swallowing a Pea at her own table, whence in a few hours she sweetly breathed her soul away into her SAVIOUR'S arms, on the 18th day of March A.D. 1780. . . ." This masterpiece of an epitaph thereupon subsides into verse. Another real prize in the way of gravestones will be found just over the brow of the hill: the pair of portrait stones of Ralph and Mary Cross. The most resonant historical associations at Old Hill are attached to the grave of Lord Timothy Dexter (1747–1806).

"Lord Timothy," elevated to the peerage by local wags, was only too happy to assume the title. Dexter had made a fortune by the timely purchase of large sums in depreciated Continental currency. He built a splendid mansion at 201 High Street in Newburyport (still standing) and filled it with statues of the world's great men, including himself; on one occasion—troubled by the thought that, when the time came, he would be unable to enjoy the glorious obsequies he so richly deserved—Dexter staged a magnificent mock funeral for himself. A book he published in 1802, *A Pickle for the Knowing Ones,* was marked by a highly individual orthography and a complete absence of punctuation. A subsequent edition contained a page of commas and periods, with the instruction that readers "pepper and salt it as they please."

St. Paul's Churchyard. [143]   On High Street.

At one side of St. Paul's Church is a small but extremely attractive collection of eighteenth-century slates. Note in particular the stone of Capt. Anthony Gwyn, shown wearing his full-dress uniform, and that of Capt. Joseph Atkins, "who (with his whole Ship's Company) perished by Shipwreck on Cape Cod Febr. the 8th, 1787."

NEW MARLBORO

New Marlboro Cemetery. [144]   Take the dirt road which leaves Route 57 at an angle, opposite the church on New Marlboro Green. The cemetery is ⅓ mile straight ahead.

Beautiful and secluded, the cemetery extends over two knolls, thought to have been Indian burial mounds; it is set about with tall pine trees. Among many interesting stones, the oldest date from the mid-eighteenth century. Note the fine marble stone of Eli Freeman (d. 1760), bearing a portrait face with wings; also the abstract sunburst design on the gravestone of Jabez Ward (d. 1786).

NORTHAMPTON

Bridge Street Cemetery. [145]   On Bridge Street (Route 9), between the center of town and the Connecticut River.

A large cemetery including stones from the seventeenth century to the present. The largest collection of old stones, mostly red sandstone, stands near the road; these are worth examining, for some are distinctly unusual. Notice for instance the curious pair of angels on the stone of Col. Seth Pomeroy, "who Died in the Army of the united States at Peekskill Febr. 19th 1777," and the splendid decorative carving on the lavishly thick stone of Mrs. Phebe Pomeroy (d. 1776).

NORTH ANDOVER

First Burying Ground. [146]   On Academy Road, ⅓ mile north of North Parish Church in the "Old Center" of North Andover.

A large number of excellent old slates in a very pretty, wooded setting: the cemetery is carefully maintained in a charming, semi-derelict condition. The oldest stone, enclosed in a granite casing, is the handsome one marking the grave of John Stevens (d. 1662). The two old cemeteries in North Andover are classic examples of intelligent and tasteful preservation.

North Parish Burying Ground. [147]   On Academy Road, fifty yards north of North Parish Church in the "Old Center" of North Andover.

Laid out in 1817. A collection of nineteenth-century stones on an impeccably-kept rectangle of ground invites the visitor to stroll through the cemetery to the back, where there is a pleasant view of the valley behind. There are trees on either side, and a neat stone wall along the road. What is quite an ordinary setting is made unusually attractive by thoughtful and painstaking treatment.

NORTHBOROUGH

Old Burial Ground. [148]   Behind the Unitarian Church; the church stands just north of Route 20, along the road marked for Boylston.

The old graveyard, now just one end of a large, modern cemetery, contains a large number of slates of extremely high quality. Evidence of a happy conjunction of money and skill can be seen in this and similar work throughout this area of Massachusetts. The stone itself, obviously of the first quality, has worn extremely well; the talented stonecutters, encouraged by generous commissions, developed styles of painstaking elegance which become pleasantly familiar as one travels from one town to the next.

Two stones in particular should not be missed. The gravestone of Deacon Mathias Rice (d. 1764) is remarkable for its great size and for its especially fine and elaborate carving. Nearby, smaller but no less beautiful, is the interesting monument to the Rabbi Judah Monis—easily spotted by its splendid skull-and-crossbones. Rabbi Monis (d. 1764 ae. 81) was Hebrew Instructor at Harvard College; in 1722 he was converted to Christianity and "publickly baptiz'd." This history gives rise to considerable exultation in the epitaph, which features this undisguisedly proselytizing verse:

A native branch of Jacob see!
Which, once from off its olive brok,
Regrafted, from the living tree   Rom. xi. 17–24
Of the reviving sap partook.

From teeming Zion's fertile womb   Isai. lxvi. 8.
As dewy drops in early morn,   Psal. cx. 3.
Or rising bodies from the tomb,   John v. 28, 29
At once be Isr'els nation born!   Isai. lxvi. 8.

NORTH READING

Harmony Vale Cemetery. [149]   On Chestnut Street, ¼ mile east of Haverhill Street.

This small and pretty private cemetery of the nineteenth century is an unexpected enclave in its setting of unbroken suburbia. In the far corner is a granite obelisk in memory of George Frederick Root (1820–95), a noted composer of popular songs: best known are his Civil War songs, "The Battle Cry of Freedom" and "Tramp, Tramp, Tramp, the Boys are Marching."

PELHAM

Knights Cemetery. [150]   On Packardville Road, just west of Route 202. Packardville Road crosses Route 202 one mile north of the town line between Pelham and Belchertown.

A small cemetery which is famous for one remarkable gravestone. It is true: the stone exists, standing quietly in the northwest corner.

WARREN GIBBS
died by arsensic poison
Mar. 23. 1860.
AE. 36 yrs. 5 mos.
23 days.

Think my friends when this you see
How my wife hath dealt by me
She in some oysters did prepare
Some poison for my lot and share
When of the same I did partake

NEWBURYPORT

And nature yielded to its fate.
Before she my wife became
Mary Felton was her name.
Erected by his Brother
WM. GIBBS.

PEPPERELL

Walton Cemetery. [151]   On Park Street, in the center of the village.

Walton Cemetery is large and varied, in use from the eighteenth century to the present day; its shady grounds have a charming setting in the attractive, peaceful town of Pepperell. These physical advantages are matched by a large number of superb slates, making a visit here most rewarding.

The old stones exhibit an unusually wide variety of carving styles: there are excellent examples of "individualized" cherubim, of the geometric style, and of an uncommon type decorated almost exclusively by intricate filigree work. The stones of the numerous Shattuck family seem to be exceptionally good.

The epitaphs here are equally worth attention. There appears to have been a kind of vogue for the graphic description of accidental death. Thus we have

——Deacon David Blood, "who was struck dead in the 70th year of his age, by an overturn of his cart" (1787)

——Aaron Bowers, "who was instantly killed by a stock of boards, Sept. 12, 1791, AEt 2 yrs. & 10 mos." The illustration on this stone depicts the accident in an abstract way.

——Lt. Joseph Farrar, "who was instantly killed by a fall in his Mill" (1802)

——Neh'h. Hobart (d. 1789 ae. 72), "whose death was caused by falling backwards, on a stick, as he was loading wood. Nobody present, but his grandson, who lived with him. . . . A kind husband, a tender parent, a trusty friend, respectable in his day, his death remarcable!"

PETERSHAM

Center Burying Ground. [152] On Route 32, east of Petersham Common.

There are a number of interesting stones on this attractive, shady hillside. A comparative rarity is the intricate carving found on several granite stones of the 1780's and '90's. Toward the back of the cemetery, notice the large slate of Dr. John Flint (d. 1810), a Freemason, with its long and flowery epitaph. Near the front a small slate "In Memo. of Eliakim Spooner (Only Child of Mr. Eliakim Spooner & Bathsheba his Wife)" (d. 1776 ae. 6) reveals at the bottom, where it has emerged from the ground, the price of the finished stone: £4.10.0, a substantial sum.

PITTSFIELD

Pittsfield Cemetery. [153] Wahconah Street (Wahconah Street is marked as Route 7 southbound; northbound traffic on Route 7 is directed through Pittsfield by another way).

The Pittsfield Cemetery was dedicated in 1850 in elaborate nineteenth-century style. Oliver Wendell Holmes was present at the opening ceremonies and read a poem composed for the occasion. It began,

> Angel of Death! Extend thy silent reign!
> Stretch thy dark sceptre o'er this new domain!

The cemetery is large and is still in use. The most interesting monuments are in the older section, some distance from the gate.

Of the two obelisks standing together on a knoll, the smaller, marble one marks the grave of the Rev. Thomas Allen (1743–1810), known as "The Fighting Parson" at the Battle of Bennington. The second obelisk, much larger and in red granite, is a memorial to his grandson, Thomas Allen (1813–82), who made a vast fortune speculating in railway shares after the Civil War. (The Cemetery's monumental gateway of piled gray stone was built in 1884 "by bequest of Thomas Allen.")

A small granite stone to William B. Look, d. 1888, is decorated with an engraving of a locomotive and tender and bears the legend, "The faithful engineer who died at his post." Look, a resident of Great Barrington, was through no fault of his own involved in a head-on collision on the Housatonic Line, as the local branch of the New Haven was called. He died in his cab, doubtless trying to stop his train, when other members of the train crews had jumped to safety.

Toward the back of the cemetery, easily distinguished, is the splendid mausoleum built for himself and family by Gordon McKay (1821–1903). McKay became very wealthy from his inventions of shoemaking machinery; he constructed this tomb ten years before his death. The outside walls are of white marble, fifteen inches thick; the interior surfaces, which can be seen dimly through the door, are finished in pink marble; the stained glass windows were exhibited in Chicago at the Columbian Exposition of 1893 before being shipped to Pittsfield. McKay left an estate of $25 million to Harvard University. Harvard University maintains the McKay mausoleum.

P L Y M O U T H

Burial Hill. [154]   Just west of (up the hill from) Route 3A
in the center of town: behind the First Church and the Church
of the Pilgrimage.

Burial Hill in Plymouth enjoys, without question, the most
magnificent site of any cemetery in New England. At the top
of the hill were established the first meeting house, the old
fort, and the watch house: from here there is a panoramic
view of Massachusetts Bay, framed by the domes and spires of
the buildings below. A map of the Bay is provided, as well as a
working drinking fountain.

The locations of the earlier buildings are indicated by signs,
and the graves of important persons are carefully marked.
These include a monument to Governor William Bradford
(1590–1657) and other graves of the eight "undertakers" of
the Plymouth Colony. Among many fine stones, perhaps the
most interesting of all is that of Patience Watson (d. 1767),
located somewhat north of the map and just east of the path
along the crest of the hill. This is a portrait stone, remarkable
in that the portrait is far more life-like (and distinctly more
attractive) than is usually the case.

P R O V I N C E T O W N

Oldest Cemetery. [155]   On Shank Painter Road, east of
Bradford Street.

The old cemetery at Provincetown is potentially interesting,
but it stands today in a sad state of disrepair. It is regrettable
that the Town of Provincetown, otherwise so attentive to its
tourist attractions, does not manage to expend a little effort
in keeping up its Oldest Cemetery.

Of topographical interest, and most unusual for New England, is the fact that this cemetery lies on a partially-covered sand dune. Where the grass no longer holds the sand together, many stones have simply toppled over. There remain several monuments of particular interest. One is a granite memorial to the four *Mayflower* passengers who died while the vessel lay in Provincetown harbor in December, 1620. Another is the fine stone, now set in granite, of Mrs. Bethiah Nickerson, d. January 26, 1806, ae. 24, and Capt. Isaiah Nickerson, "who was drownded at Bonavesta May 26, 1806," ae. 29.

QUINCY

Hancock Cemetery. [156] On Hancock Street, at Quincy Center.

An old cemetery, established in the 1640's, of considerable historic and artistic significance. It is attractive and well kept, provided with benches, and serves in effect as a small park for the center of Quincy. At the gate is a list of fifty Revolutionary soldiers buried within. Noted individuals buried here include the Rev. John Hancock (father of the patriot), Leonard Hoar (c. 1630–1675), the third president of Harvard, and various members of the Adams and Quincy families. The stones themselves include good examples of seventeenth- and early eighteenth-century styles.

Both John Adams and John Quincy Adams, together with their wives, are buried in a crypt below the First Parish Church, directly across the street. When the front doors of the church are closed, access to the presidential tombs may be had through the church office on the north side of the building. The church itself was constructed in 1828 of Quincy granite: the stone, except the columns in front, was the gift of John Adams. The handsome interior is worth a visit.

NEWBURYPORT

REHOBOTH

Burial Place Hill. [157] At the intersection of Providence, Peckham, and Mason Streets.

It is fiendishly difficult to find one's way around in the Town of Rehoboth. There is no central village to speak of, and many of the roads are unmarked. But Burial Place Hill is such an attractive cemetery that it is worth taking some trouble to get there: keep asking directions until you find it.

The cemetery occupies a small hill above the level of the road. It is a beautiful site, carefully maintained. Toward the front are a number of very fine stones dating from the eighteenth century. At the back is the tomb of Simeon Martin, a nineteenth-century Lieutenant Governor of Rhode Island, with an unusually lengthy epitaph recounting his varied career. There is a very curious, self-pitying epitaph on the stone of Seth J. Miller (d. 1848), complaining of the treachery of his wife and children. One wonders who paid for the monument.

RICHMOND

Richmond Center Cemetery. [158] On Route 41.

Established in 1765, the same year as the town; contains the graves of early settlers and of Revolutionary soldiers. The Richmond cemetery also contains two monuments distinctly out of the ordinary. Near the gate an obelisk marks the grave of Hiram Fairbanks, a track superintendant, killed by a train wreck in 1851: the wreck is depicted in relief on the stone. Elsewhere is the grave of Florella Perry, d. 1807, "who being dead, still forcibly, though silently, repeats her dying admonition, 'Prepare for death.' "

SALEM

The Burying Point. [159] Charter Street, near the town center.

Amid the somewhat bleak surroundings of an urban renewal district, Salem's old cemetery is nevertheless outstanding in the historical interest and quality of its stones. A bronze plaque near the entrance provides a key to the location of the more noteworthy graves. Among those buried here are Simon Bradstreet, a colonial governor of Massachusetts; his wife Anne Bradstreet (1612?–72), who wrote the first American poetry that anybody still reads; and Justice John Hathorne, one of the judges of the Salem witch trials.

Another grave indicated by the plaque is that of Nathanael Mather (d. 1688): it bears the inscription, "An Aged person that had seen but Nineteen Winters in the World." Precocious Nathanael, son of Increase Mather and brother of Cotton Mather, had entered Harvard College at the age of twelve. Among many fine examples of stonecutting note in particular the elaborate stone of Timothy Lindall (d. 1698), with a skeleton and a figure of Time on either side.

Toward the northeast corner is a large old willow tree: its trunk has wholly or partly enveloped at least four gravestones.

SANDWICH

Old Town Cemetery. [160] On Grove Street, which runs south from Route 130 by the town hall.

A very attractive setting on a small head of land jutting into Shawme Pond: ducks may be seen wandering among the stones. In the center of the graveyard is one monument of particular interest: this is a square marble pillar in memory of "Capt. James L. Nye of Sandwich, who was killed by a whale in the Pacific Ocean Dec. 29, 1852, while in command of the Bark Andrew of New Bedford. . . ."

SHEFFIELD

Barnard Cemetery. [161]   On Route 7, south of the village.

A pleasant, roadside cemetery, worth a brief stop. The attraction here is a number of fine, extra-large marble tablets. Toward the back, note the markers of Mrs. Mary and Miss Cynthia Hickok. Best of all, slightly to the south side, is the marker of Gen. John Fellows (d. 1808). The remarkable engraving depicts the General as an angel winging his way to heaven.

Bow Wow Cemetery. [162]   On Bow Wow Road: turn west from Route 7 at the corner next to the Sheffield Grille; follow this road's turnings for 3⅕ miles, at which point the pavement ends; proceed *straight ahead* an additional ½ mile.

A modest cemetery, pleasantly secluded, the older section surrounded by tall pine trees. One gravestone, recently replaced by a replica in heavy slate, carries a noteworthy epitaph. Beneath it lies Mr. Simon Willard, who "was instantly killed. Oct. 19. 1766."

> Stop here ye Gay
> & ponder what ye doath
> Blue Lightnings Flew &
> swiftly seized my Breath
> A more tremendous
> Flash will fill the skies
> When I and all that
> Sleep in death shall rise.

Several of the older stones are decorated with an attractive sunflower design.

S H E L B U R N E

Hill Cemetery. [163] Turn north off Route 2 near the Congregational Church in Shelburne Center. A little less than half a mile along, take the right-hand fork onto Old Village Road, which runs sharply uphill. The cemetery is at the top of the hill.

Provides a hilltop setting and a large number of old slates of the eighteenth and nineteenth centuries. Near the front are three slate stones, each of which marks the graves of *two* children of Deacon John and Mrs. Mary Barnard. These include two sons, both named Job; twin sons, Moses and Aaron, who died within a week of their birth; and two daughters, Joanna and Mary. On each stone are engraved the figures of the children lying in their coffins.

S H U T E S B U R Y

Shutesbury Cemetery. [164] West of the village center, on the road to Leverett.

A pleasant cemetery of no great antiquity, on a knoll among tall pine trees. Near the top of the knoll is a small marble marker inscribed as follows:

Erected by the Town of Shutesbury in memory of
EPHRIAM PRATT
Born in East Sudbury Nov. 1. 1686. Removed to Shutesbury soon after its first settlement where he resided until he Died May 22. 1804. IN HIS 117 YEAR. He was remarkably

cheerful in his disposition and temperate in his habits. He swung a scythe 101 consecutive years and mounted a horse without assistance at the age of 110.

SOUTH CHELMSFORD

Hart Pond Cemetery. [165] On Parkerville Road: turn west from Route 27 at the post office.

A cemetery of distinct but modest charms: worth a stop though not a detour. It has a pleasant setting within a white picket fence, across from Hart Pond. Dating mainly from the nineteenth century, it contains a number of interesting stones: the best of these is near the center, a large slate "ERECTED By a Number of Friends In Memory of Hosea Procter who died March the 6th 1796; aged 19 years." There follows a touching epitaph, beginning "O Procter, friend of Virtue, wisdom, truth. . . ."

SPRINGFIELD

Springfield Cemetery. [166] The main entrance is at the end of Cemetery Avenue, which begins at 171 Maple Street, south of the city center.

A large urban cemetery with several monuments which are worth looking for. Most of the elaborate ones are together on the Cedar Street side. Here may be seen the amazing monument to the Titus family—an attractive two-story family dwelling, six feet high, executed in white marble. The house bears the motto, "In Mansions Above." On the Pine Street side is a collection of eighteenth-century markers in red sandstone, brought here from earlier graveyards. A short distance

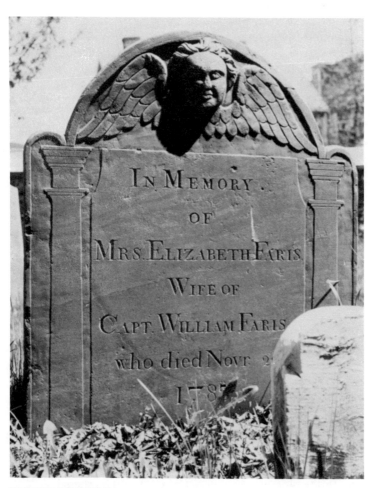

IN MEMORY
OF
MRS. ELIZABETH FARIS
WIFE OF
CAPT. WILLIAM FARIS
who died Novr. 2
1787

NEWBURYPORT

west of these, in a plot set off by stone posts in the form of a cannon, is the large red sandstone tomb of Capt. William Day (1715–97). One side depicts a sea battle he fought with the French in the Bay of Biscay "about the year 1760." The other side gives a full account of the engagement. On the hill at the north end of the cemetery is a monument to Josiah G. Holland (1819–81), an author and sometime editor of the Springfield *Republican*. The bronze relief bust of Mr. Holland is the work of Augustus Saint-Gaudens.

STERLING

Chocksett Cemetery. [167]   On Route 62, just east of the village center.

A charming and beautiful old cemetery, rising and falling over a series of mounds, with a picturesque mixture of black slate and white marble stones. Its name recalls the origins of the town, which began as the Chocksett Parish of the Town of Lancaster. The first settler, Gamaliel Beaman (d. 1745), came here in 1720. Most of the oldest and most interesting stones are in the area nearest the road: there are numerous eighteenth-century slates, some of them very fine.

STOCKBRIDGE

Center Cemetery. [168]   Main and Church Streets, across from the town hall.

An exceptionally interesting cemetery on a handsome wooded site. In the oldest section, near Church Street, is the table-stone monument to the Rev. John Sergeant (d. 1749), a colonial missionary to the Stockbridge Indians; many of the Indians

138

whom he converted were buried around him. Sergeant's remarkable epitaph is believed to have been composed by his
friend Capt. John Konkapot, chief of the Stockbridge Indians.

> Where is that pleasing Form, I ask, thou canst
> not show;
> He's not within, false stone, There's nought
> but Dust below;
> And where's that pious soul, that Thinking
> conscious MIND?
> Wilt thou pretend, vain cypher, THAT's with thee
> enshrined?
> Alas, my Friend's not here with thee that I can find;
> Here's not a Sergeant's body or a Sergeant's MIND.
> I'll seek him hence, for all's alike Deception here.
> I'll go to Heav'n & I shall find my Sergeant there.

Near to this is the grave of Brig. Gen. Moses Ashley, "who
being in perfect health and in the midst of public business,
died in a sudden and unexpected manner August 25, 1791."

There is fine carving on many of the stones in the older
areas. Near the Main Street side, for instance, note the adjacent
stones of Miss Lydia Dix and Mr. Silas Bingham. The former
is extremely simple, with an elegant sunburst design; the latter
is elaborate, with a curious representation of the soul flying to
heaven.

At the end of the central driveway is the secluded plot of
the famous Sedgwick family, with its stones set in concentric
circles. Among many grander monuments is the grave of Elizabeth Freeman, who as an escaped slave won her freedom in
1783 under the Massachusetts Bill of Rights. The lawyer who
handled her case was Theodore Sedgwick, and Elizabeth Freeman came to work as a free woman for the Sedgwick family.
Her burial within the family circle demonstrates to what

extent she was beloved. The epitaph was written by Catharine Maria Sedgwick (1789–1867), a noted novelist: Miss Sedgwick was the author of a series of domestic novels set in the Berkshires, including *The Linwoods* and *Married or Single,* the latter a defense of her decision not to marry.

Elizabeth Freeman
Known by the name of
Mum Bet
died Dec. 28, 1829

Her supposed age was 85 years.
She was born a slave and
remained a slave for nearly
thirty years. She could neither
read nor write yet in
her own sphere she had no
superior nor equal. She neither
wasted time nor property.
She never violated a trust nor
failed to perform a duty.
In every situation of domestic
trial she was the most efficient
helper, and the tenderest friend.
Good Mother, farewell.

STURBRIDGE

Old Burying Ground. [169]   At the end of Sturbridge Common, on Route 131.

The old graveyard at Sturbridge has a beautiful setting on a wooded hillside. It is enclosed by a stone wall which—according to tradition—was built by four companies of Sturbridge Revolutionary soldiers, each company building one side.

There are many fine stones, primarily slate. Near the southeast corner, however, one of the most beautiful items is a
small marker in red sandstone at the grave of Lovice Dunten
(d. 1786). Not far away is a marble stone, decorated with a
precariously leaning willow tree, "In memory of Mr. Benjamin
Goodell, who was instantly killed by the falling of a tree, Feb.
19th. 1801. . . ."

TEWKSBURY

Old Center Burying Ground. [170] On East Street, which
runs off Main Street (Route 38) from a point near the bandstand.

The "Old Center" is one of two cemeteries opposite each other
on East Street. Both are attractive, though the smaller and
older graveyard has the more interesting stones. In the first
row of these is the grave of Lt. William Kittredge, d. 1789 ae.
92, with the following epitaph:

> He's gone at length, how many grieve!
> Whom he did gen'rously relieve.
> But O how shocking he expire
> Amidst the flames of raging fire!
> Yet all who sleep in Christ are bless'd
> Whatever way they are undress'd.

TOPSFIELD

Pine Grove Cemetery. [171] On Route 97, ½ mile north of
the village green.

This attractive, well-kept cemetery was laid out in 1663 and
has been in continuous use ever since. The older, original

section contains several items of particular interest. A brown-stone obelisk marks the graves of several of the ancestors of Joseph Smith (1805–44), founder of the Mormon Church. In a chained-off lot at the south end is a marble stone in memory of Thomas Perkins, "An eminent Merchant," d. 1830: a fine epitaph details his rags-to-riches career. Next to the Perkins lot is the handsome gravestone of Esther Dwinell, who died in 1847 aged 101 years and 8 months.

There are a number of good eighteenth-century stones. The earliest legible one is that of Capt. Thomas Baker (d. 1718). The most remarkable by all odds is that of Mrs. Mary Lefavour, d. 1797 ae. 74. It stands not far from a fenced-in plot near the entrance. The epitaph is as follows:

> Reader pass on, ne'er waste your time
> On bad biography, and bitter rhyme.
> For what I am, this umb'rous clay ensures,
> And what I was, is no affair of yours.
> Erected by Amos Lefavour

TRURO

First Congregational Parish Churchyard. [172]   Behind the church, on Town Hall Road.

There is nothing remarkable about this quiet churchyard: the church itself dates from 1827 and the graves are no older. Still, the setting is isolated, peaceful, and unusually pretty, and many people will feel this pleasant spot is worth a visit.

UPTON

Old Town Cemetery. [173]   Just over a mile south of Route 140, the road to Mendon is joined by Grove Street. At this

SPRINGFIELD

small intersection is a boulder bearing a plaque. This marks the beginning of a footpath which was, long ago, the original road from Upton to Milford. The old cemetery lies along this path. Walk in, bear to the left of the private driveway, then continue straight ahead about fifty yards.

Finding this old cemetery, hidden away in the woods, is easy enough: but it feels like a great discovery. The woods have taken over the old clearing, and within its stone walls the cemetery is overgrown with ferns and other plants. The effect, in this case, is a very pleasant one. The stones are actually in good condition, and finding them beneath the ferns and bushes makes an enjoyable exploration. The stone walls are intact, and they show the cemetery to be surprisingly large. Among many interesting gravestones, the most striking is the excellent portrait stone of the Rev. Elisha Fish (d. 1795). Next to it, the stone of the Widow Hannah Fish, his Consort (d. 1796), is smaller but equally fine.

WATERTOWN

Old Burying Ground. [174] On Mount Auburn Street (Route 16) at Arlington Street.

Its setting in modern Watertown is no longer congenial, but this old cemetery (dating from 1642) remains an important one for its collection of stones and its historical associations. There are several seventeenth-century stones in good condition: notice the curious figures on the sides of the gravestone of Mr. John Stone (d. 1691). Members of the Coolidge and Garfield families buried here were ancestors, respectively, of those U.S. presidents.

WEST BARNSTABLE

West Barnstable Cemetery. [175] On Route 6A, at the junction with Route 149.

A very attractive graveyard, planted with carefully trimmed yew trees: it contains several stones of particular historical interest. By the wall on the east side are graves of the Otis family, including the fine stone of James Otis (d. 1778), father of James Otis the orator and patriot. It bears an elegant epitaph about patriotism, very likely written by his famous son, which concludes on a strangely diffident note:

> Exchanged this TEMPORAL EXISTENCE
> we trust
> For A HAPPY ETERNITY, Novr 9th 1778
> Spes & fortuna valete,
> sat me ludistis;
> Ludite nunc alios.

Another interesting epitaph—this one extraordinarily flowery —will be found on the marble obelisk nearby, in memory of Maria Otis Colby (d. 1821). A plaque on the outside wall directs the visitor to the grave of Capt. John "Mad Jack" Percival (1779–1862), who commanded the U.S.S. *Constitution* on a voyage around the world in 1844–46.

The famous frigate, known as "Old Ironsides," has enjoyed as many lives as are given to any half-dozen cats. Commissioned in 1798, she first served in the Tripolitan War; during the War of 1812 she won several notable victories, defeating the British ships *Guerrière* and *Java* in battles that are famous to this day. Some years later the ship was condemned as unseaworthy, but a public outcry, spurred by Oliver Wendell Holmes' poem "Old Ironsides," led to her reprieve. All told, "Old Ironsides" was rebuilt in 1833, 1877, and 1925—the last time by public subscription. She has fought forty battles and never lost one. The *Constitution* can be visited today at the Charlestown Navy Yard in Boston.

WESTON

Farmers' Burying Ground. [176]   On the Boston Post Road in the center of the village, at the head of Concord Road.

An extremely handsome village cemetery, immaculately kept. There are several excellent eighteenth-century stones, distinguished by fine "individualized" cherubim. The most famous man buried here is Samuel Phillips Savage, leader of the Massachusetts Board of War in the Revolution. Savage was a friend of John Adams; he is thought to have been one of the organizers of the Boston Tea Party.

WEST STERLING

Leg Cemetery. [177]   On Route 140, two miles south of Route 62.

The chief interest of this small cemetery, in the front row, is the stone of Robert B. Thomas (d. 1846 ae. 80). Thomas was the original editor and publisher of *The Old Farmers' Almanac.* He was a schoolmaster in Sterling, and published the first edition of his almanac in 1793.

WOBURN

Ancient Burying Ground. [178]   On Park Street, approximately behind the First Baptist Church at the center of town. The cemetery, which is kept locked, is maintained for the Town of Woburn by the Woodbrook Cemetery Association. Arrangements to visit the Ancient Burying Ground may be made by telephoning the Association at (617) 933-0297.

As may be judged by the instructions above, a visit to Woburn's old graveyard requires some forethought; but for those interested in the intricate early carving styles, the riches of the stones here will more than adequately repay the trouble. The interesting contract arrangement by which the Burying Ground is maintained results, unfortunately, in a locked gate— but it must be said that the grounds are immaculately kept and some of the old and rare stones are wonderfully well preserved.

The chief historical and artistic interest lies in the group of old stones slightly to the left of the entrance, apparently set in no order but turned every which way. The low profile of these stones immediately identifies them as early ones: they date from the very end of the seventeenth and beginning of the eighteenth century. Typical is the stone of the Rev. Jabez Fox (d. 1703), which incorporates in its design every symbol from a skull to a border of fertility emblems. Notice the dual portrait heads on the sides. Nearby stones show interesting variations of the same elements.

The cemetery itself dates from 1642, the year of Woburn's first settlement. Among those buried here may be traced more or less distant ancestors of Presidents Pierce, Cleveland, Benjamin Harrison, and Franklin Roosevelt.

Several of the epitaphs are rewarding. Of one stone only the bottom half remains, with the epitaph on the nameless family:

> These deaths are much to be observ'd:
> Such Instances are scarce heard off.
> Six weeping Children in Eight Days
> followed Father & Mother to their Graves. . . .

But the prize inscription will be found on a tablet standing next to the one table stone in the cemetery. This marks the grave of Mrs. Elizabeth Cotton, "Who Died a V I R G I N October 12th 1742 AEtatis 46."

> If a Virgin Marry She hath not Sinned
> Nevertheless Such shall have trouble in the Flesh
> But He that giveth her not in Marriage doth better
> She is happier if She so Abide.

W O O D S   H O L E

Church of the Messiah Churchyard. [179]   Church Street.

The old section of this churchyard is extremely small, and it cannot be recommended to those whose interest lies primarily in the historical aspects of cemeteries. Nevertheless this is an unusually attractive example of a small, modern cemetery. It has a fine hillside setting. A number of recent gravestones have· been executed in black slate with decorative emblems of modern design: this is distinctly unusual, since most slate stones produced now (and they are rare enough) are either completely plain or imitate earlier styles. One recent granite monument bears a large engraving of a fishing boat.

W O R C E S T E R

Common Burying Ground. [180]   In the eastern part of the Common: occupies an area running to the northwest from Salem Square, approximately as far as the Bigelow Monument.

Worcester's Common Burying Ground is an invisible cemetery. Many graveyards in New England, long since abandoned, have become virtually impossible to find; but Worcester's earliest burying ground, easily located in the center of town, is an example of a cemetery that was consciously and intentionally ploughed under.

HERE LIES BURIED
Ye BODY OF Mrs
EUNICE SAWYER
Ye WIFE OF Lieut
EPHRIAM SAWYER
WHO DECd
JUNE 24th
A·D 1748
AGE 52 YEARS

STERLING

Burials took place in Worcester Common from 1728 to 1824: the burying ground was thereafter neglected. In 1853 the City Council, with no time for such tomfoolery as "preservation," ordered the stones laid flat and covered with two feet of earth. The location of the stones was established in 1966, after considerable research, by Daniel Farber and Charles Bouley; some experimental excavations demonstrated that the gravestones are all in place, twenty-four to thirty inches below the ground, with the carving preserved in excellent condition.

Hope Cemetery. [181]   On Webster Street (Route 12), south of the city center.

A large, nineteenth-century cemetery with several notable monuments. Near the main entrance is a marble obelisk erected by the descendants of Peter Slater, who as a fourteen-year-old ropemaker's apprentice was the youngest participant in the Boston Tea Party. Further into the grounds are two of the set pieces of this style of cemetery, both of them realized unusually well: these are a particularly fine Firemen's Memorial (1896) and an Odd Fellows' lot marked by a massive ball and three huge links of chain in red granite. One section contains a large number of stones in green slate, dating from the early nineteenth century, which were moved from their original location on the Common. In a newer section, on higher ground, is the grave of Dr. Robert H. Goddard (1882–1945), the inventor of the liquid-fuel rocket. The hills from which Dr. Goddard launched experimental rockets are visible in the distance.

NEW HAMPSHIRE

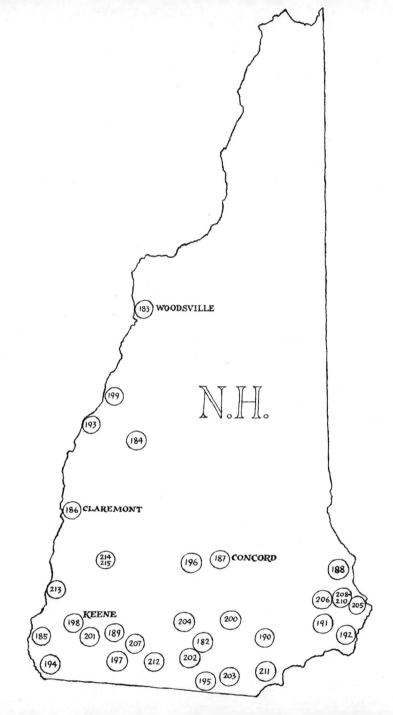

182. Amherst
183. Bath
184. Canaan Center
185. Chesterfield
186. Claremont
187. Concord
188. Dover
189. Dublin
190. East Derry
191. Exeter
192. Hampton
193. Hanover
194. Hinsdale
195. Hollis
196. Hopkinton
197. Jaffrey Center

198. Keene
199. Lyme
200. Manchester
201. Marlborough
202. Milford
203. Nashua
204. New Boston
205. New Castle
206. Newmarket
207. Peterborough
208–210. Portsmouth
211. Salem
212. Temple
213. Walpole
214, 215. Washington

MARLBOROUGH

Sure, if I reprehend anything in this world, it is the use of my oracular tongue, and a nice derangement of epitaphs.

MRS. MALAPROP

AMHERST

Oldest Cemetery. [182]   Beside the town hall at the north end of the common.

A quiet, well-kept cemetery in a picturesque village setting. Several of the old stones are worth particular notice. Close behind the town hall is an impressive table stone erected by the town in memory of the Rev. Daniel Wilkins (d. 1783) : in many small towns, the most elaborate stones were erected at public expense to mark the graves of the local pastors. Near to this is an interesting marker for Col. John Shepherd (d. 1785) ; and at the back, among the trees, is a large and hand-some stone for the Hon. Moses Nichols (d. 1790) .

BATH

Old Cemetery. [183]   On Route 302, just north of the village.

The older stones in this roadside cemetery are worth a brief stop. There is a large and handsome slate at the grave of Jeremiah Hutchins (d. 1816) , "—being one of the first settlers in Bath, from a wilderness, he rais'd a flourishing village—then died respected, as he lived beloved." Nearby are several rough homemade stones dating from the 1790's. At one end of the cemetery is an interesting example of the fancy ironwork gates that were sometimes used for fenced-off family plots. In this case the plot is marked off by granite pillars, but no stones were ever placed within.

CANAAN CENTER

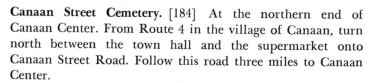

Canaan Street Cemetery. [184] At the northern end of Canaan Center. From Route 4 in the village of Canaan, turn north between the town hall and the supermarket onto Canaan Street Road. Follow this road three miles to Canaan Center.

An agreeable spot, to be recommended less for its monuments than for its physical setting. Across the street stands the handsome Old North Church, built in 1828. To the northwest, beyond the cemetery, stretches a very impressive view of the White Mountains. The stones are appropriate but not exceptional.

CHESTERFIELD

Village Burying Ground. [185] Behind the town hall, in the center of the village.

A small, attractive graveyard with stones dating back to the 1770's. Note the triple headstone for the three children of Ensign Zenas Fairbank, all d. 1786. The stone of Leah Day notes that "her first husband was Lt. Amos Hubbard." Lt. Hubbard is buried on one side of her, Mr. Day on the other.

CLAREMONT

West Claremont Burying Ground. [186]   Opposite the Union Church (Episcopal) in West Claremont. Driving through the village of West Claremont on Route 103, watch for the "Episcopal Church Welcomes You" sign which indicates the road leading south, across the Sugar River, to the church.

The land for this, the first cemetery in Claremont, was voted by the town in 1768. Inside a small iron railing is the oldest stone, marking the grave of Mr. Benadick Roys (d. 1769). In the original section is a grove of huge pine trees which have swallowed up several of the stones. Over the years the cemetery has become very extensive, and it is now preponderantly modern.

Union Church, across the street, was erected in 1771: it is the oldest Episcopal Church in New Hampshire. Within the new part of the cemetery is Old St. Mary, the first Roman Catholic church in New Hampshire. The small, handsome brick structure was built in 1823.

CONCORD

Old North Cemetery. [187]   On North State Street, near Bouton Street, north of the city center.

The earliest settlers of Concord are buried here, though few of the oldest stones remain. There is however a charming portrait stone erected by the town in memory of the Rev. Timothy Walker (d. 1782).

Toward the back of the grounds is a separate enclosure, surrounded by its own iron fence. Within it is buried Franklin Pierce (1804–69), fourteenth President of the United States.

DOVER

Pine Hill Cemetery. [188]   On Central Avenue (Route 16), south of the town center.

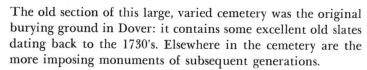

The old section of this large, varied cemetery was the original burying ground in Dover: it contains some excellent old slates dating back to the 1730's. Elsewhere in the cemetery are the more imposing monuments of subsequent generations.

DUBLIN

Town Cemetery. [189]   On Route 101 at Old Common Road, west of the village; opposite Dublin Lake.

The original town cemetery, established in 1751; it is next to the site of the first meeting house, in an attractive setting across from the lake. The oldest stones are at the back, away from the modern highway. Two interesting table stones carry lengthy epitaphs to the Rev. Edward Sprague, second pastor of the Church of Dublin, and his wife. By the stone wall along the old road is the grave of F. Nelson Blount (d. 1967), the founder of "Steamtown," the railroad museum in Bellows Falls, Vermont: it is marked by a granite monument engraved with a fine 2-6-0 steam locomotive.

EAST DERRY

Forest Hill Cemetery. [190]   On the hill behind the Congregational Church.

A large, attractively wooded, hilltop cemetery containing in all nearly four hundred graves from colonial times. A signpost directs visitors to the grave of the Rev. James McGregore (d. 1729), the first citizen of the Scotch-Irish settlement known originally as Londonderry. Next to it is a large and extremely elegant portrait stone at the grave of his son, the Rev. David Macgregore (d. 1777).

Among numerous interesting stones, the real prize is the marker of Dr. Philip Godfird Kast: it stands encased in cement, just east of the central drive. Dr. Kast died, one would judge, in the second half of the eighteenth century; the exact date was never filled in. The stone is engraved with elab symbolism, including the sun, moon, and stars amid various Masonic paraphernalia.

EXETER

Winter Street Cemetery. [191]   On Winter Street at Front Street (Route 111).

An old cemetery, once very attractive, now in considerable disrepair. The most notable graves are on the west side, those of the numerous and distinguished Gilman family: they include Nicholas Gilman, a signer of the Federal Constitution for New Hampshire, and John T. Gilman, a Governor of New Hampshire. Also among them is Mrs. Tabitha Tenney (1762–1837), a daughter of Samuel Gilman, who has some claim to be the first woman novelist in America. Mrs. Tenney's most popular work was *Female Quixotism: Exhibited in the*

JAFFREY

Romantic Opinions and Extravagant Adventures of Dorcasina Sheldon, of which the following is a representative extract.

Here Dorcasina could contain herself no longer. "I had thought, sir," said she, hesitating, "I had expected from your professions, a quite different reception from this." "Did you, indeed? Gad, my dear, you are in the right." Upon this he threw his arms round her neck, and almost stifled her with kisses. The astonished Dorcasina endeavored to disengage herself, but in vain; for the enraptured barber continued his caresses, only at intervals, exclaiming, "Gad, my dear, how happy we shall be when we are married. I shall love you infinitely, I am sure." Dorcasina, at length, finding breath, in a loud and angry tone, exclaimed, "Let me go this moment; unhand me, sir. I will not endure to be thus treated."

HAMPTON

Pine Grove Cemetery. [192]   On Winnacummet Road, ½ mile east of Route 1.

This handsome graveyard dates from 1642, though the very oldest stones have been either removed or buried under centuries' accumulation of pine needles. Most of those remaining are of the eighteenth century. Note the large slate monument to the Rev. Ebenezer Thayer.

HANOVER

Dartmouth Cemetery. [193]   Directly west of the central campus: the main entrance is at the western end of Sanborn Lane, which runs west from North Main Street between McNutt Hall and Robinson Hall.

The college cemetery stands on college land, a short walk from the main quadrangle; yet it is charmingly secluded in a peaceful, wooded setting. Aside from its physical attractions, what is unusually interesting is that this was plainly the community burying ground for the small, isolated community of Dartmouth College in its early years. Students were buried here, as well as faculty and college presidents: not a few died of consumption during the long winter months. The rows of stones which trace this pattern of disease are a grim suggestion of the *vox clamantis in deserto.*

Near the entrance is the tomb of the founder of the college, Eleazar Wheelock (d. 1779), and of his wife Mary (d. 1783). Nearby are many graves of faculty and students. Several of the most interesting markers were erected by various fraternities and social clubs in memory of their departed fellows.

HINSDALE

Hooker Cemetery. [194]　South of the elementary and high schools, which lie west of the village on Route 119. Drive in past the high school; behind it turn right, and watch for a turnstile at the edge of a field. The cemetery is across the field at the edge of the woods.

A most attractive setting at the edge of the woods, shaded by beautiful old trees. A huge maple tree near the entrance has surrounded with its roots or partially enveloped a dozen stones, one of them the mournful tablet of Miss Cynthia Cooper, d. 1800 ae. 25—"Reader, attend, while I rehearse / My dismal fate set forth in verse." She does so, at considerable length. Further back is a fine table-stone monument to Col. Ebenezer Hinsdale (d. 1765), with an inscription referring to the Colonel's "supernatural endowments."

H O L L I S

Congregational Churchyard. [195] Behind the Congregational Church at the center of the village.

A small graveyard, crowded with eighteenth-century graves. The town's prosperity at that period is demonstrated by the proliferation of exceptionally large, exceptionally fine slate markers. Certain stones should not be missed. The marker of William Cumings Atwel (d. 1778 ae. 15) describes his accidental death: "This misfortunate Youth was mortally wounded by falling & being caught under a Sled deeply Laden with wood about 48 hours befor his Death to the Great Grief of his Affectionate Parents. Mors miseretu neque vivitum neque Pauperum." Note, side by side, the splendid portrait stone of the Rev Francis Worcester (d. 1783) and the stone of Mrs. Lydia Worcester (d. 1772), showing her coffin with the casket inside. Best of all is a large slate, at the far end of the yard from the church, at the grave of Dr. John Jones (d. 1796) :

> In youth he was a scholar bright,
> In learning he took great delight;
> He was a Major's only Son,
> It was for love he was undone.

H O P K I N T O N

Hopkinton Cemetery. [196]   On Route 9, next to the town hall.

The charming setting of this small cemetery invites a brief stop. There are some good eighteenth-century slates: note especially the one erected by the town in memory of the Rev. Elijah Fletcher (d. 1786) .

JAFFREY CENTER

Old Burying Ground. [197]   Out of sight of the road, behind
the Original Meeting House and its horse sheds.

A favorite cemetery with many people, distinguished by its
beautiful setting and interesting graves. The handsome spire
of the Meeting House provides a classic backdrop.

The best-known graves at Jaffrey Center are those of Amos
Fortune and his wife. Amos Fortune was a Negro slave who
bought his own and his wife's freedom; at his death he left a
sum of money to the Town of Jaffrey for the use of one of the
local schools.

SACRED	SACRED
to the memory of	to the memory of
AMOS FORTUNE	VIOLATE
who was born free in	by sale the slave of
Africa, a slave in America,	Amos Fortune, by Marri-
he purchased liberty,	age his wife; by her
professed Christianity,	fidelity his friend and
lived reputably, &	solace, she died his widow
died hopefully,	Sept. 13, 1802.
Nov. 17, 1801.	AEt. 73.
AEt. 91.	

In the northwest corner is the curious tomb constructed by
Count Viggo Brandt Erichsen for his first wife and infant
daughter. Carved in relief on the tomb's granite facade are his
wife's face and several scenes from the life of Christ. In the far
southwest corner is the grave of the novelist Willa Cather
(1876–1947). The stone carries an epitaph taken from *My
Antonia*—"that is happiness, to be dissolved into something
complete and great."

KEENE

Washington Street Cemetery. [198]   On Washington Street (Routes 9 and 10) at Mechanic Street, just north of the center of town.

Washington Street Cemetery itself has been in use since 1795, but its best stones, at the back behind the flagpole, are somewhat earlier: they were moved here in 1904 from their original location in the First Church Yard. Here is the beautiful stone of Madam Ruth Whitney (d. 1788), bearing a portrait with wings and an eloquent epitaph:

> . . . For Diligence, Patience, Piety & Knowledge
> She was eminently distinguished.
> As this Stone cannot tell all her virtues,
> Suffice it to say,   That
> As a wife she was Prudent and Faithful,
> As a mother, Discreet and Tender,
> As a Neighbour, Friendly and Charitable,
> As a Christian, Intelligent and Exemplary.
> A Life thus spent terminated with composure
> On the first of November 1788.

The adjacent stone of Mrs. Abigail Reed also deserves attention for its fine carving and epitaph.

In the first row, at the Washington Street end, is the marble stone of Seth Newcomb, d. 1811 ae. 25, "whose life, though short, was active, too much devoted, however, to the world, and too little to his maker . . .," but who, the epitaph continues, was converted during his fatal illness.

THE VEIL WILL BE LIFTED!

RICHARD TOWNE

DIED

Sept. 11, 1869.

Æ. 87.

WASHINGTON

LYME

Old Lyme Cemetery. [199] Behind the Congregational Church at the center of the village.

This neatly enclosed, attractive graveyard was established in 1786 as the town's second burial place. There are several interesting stones in the older section. The greatest human interest, however, attaches to a marble obelisk near the back which marks the graves of three young men of Lyme who died in the Civil War. Charles Lovejoy, Turner Grant, and John Gilbert were boyhood companions. In August, 1862 they went together to enlist in the Union Army; they fought together at Fredericksburg; and in March, 1863, they died at Newport News. According to local tradition, the three flag-draped caskets were found on the front porch when the family of one of the boys returned from church one Sunday. Nobody in town had received any previous notification of their deaths.

MANCHESTER

Stark Burial Plot. [200] At the bottom of Stark Park, River Road and Park Avenue, north of the center. River Road runs north from underneath the eastern end of Amoskeag Bridge.

This handsome park, above the Merrimack River, is in honor of General John Stark (1728–1822), hero of the Battle of Bennington. In the center is a fine equestrian statue of the General. At the bottom of the hill are the graves of General Stark, his wife Elizabeth (commonly known as Molly Stark), and his parents. The graves are within the Stark family burial plot: the house built by Stark formerly stood a short distance to the north. The surrounding area was purchased by the City of Manchester in 1890 for use as a park.

MARLBOROUGH

Frost Hill Cemetery. [201] On the summit of Frost Hill.
From Route 124, south of the village center, turn uphill past
the Federated Church and the Frost Library. Follow this road's
turnings (but do not turn off this road) for 1½ miles.

This isolated cemetery takes some getting to, but it is well
worth the effort. It occupies a quiet and secluded spot surrounded by woods, though the stone walls demonstrate that
this was once cultivated land. In the southwest corner, near
the road, is a group of stones of the Ward family, all exceptionally fine. Among them is the grave of Patty Ward, d. 1795, ae.
5 years, 6 months, 27 days:

> By boiling cyder she was slain
> Whilst less than six of age
> Then her exquisite racking pain
> Removed her from the stage.
> But her immortal spirit went
> To the Almighty King,
> Where all the godly ones are sent
> The praise of God to sing.

Elsewhere a small marble tablet marks the grave of Martin
Van Buren, adopted son of Nathane and Eunice Wild, d. 1845
ae. 8.

MILFORD

Old Burying Ground. [202]　On the north side of Elm Street (Route 101), just west of the town center.

In the back row of this cemetery, close to the entrance, is a marble gravestone belonging to the category of notable curiosities. It marks the grave of Caroline H., Wife of Calvin Cutter, M.D., "Murdered by the Baptist Ministry & Baptist Churches as follows:—Sept. 28, 1838. . . ." The harangue that comprises the epitaph is very difficult to decipher; the gist of it is that Mrs. Cutter was accused in church of lying, and was prevented from clearing her name to her satisfaction. It concludes: "The intentional and malicious destruction of her character & happiness, as above described, destroyed her life. Her last words upon the subject were 'tell the truth, & the iniquity will come out.' "

　　In front of this unhappy monument is a plaque in memory of Carrie Cutter, a daughter of Dr. Cutter by his second wife. At the age of nineteen, Carrie Cutter volunteered to serve as an assistant nurse in the Union Navy; not long thereafter she died of fever. "She was the first female to enter the service of her country in the Civil War, the first that fell at her post, and the first to form organized efforts to supply the sick of the army."

NASHUA

Old South Cemetery. [203]　South of the city, on the west side of the Daniel Webster Highway (Route 3); the cemetery is one mile north of the Massachusetts line.

Old South Cemetery comes as a pleasant surprise. It is a long way from the center of town, and it stands amid the familiar roadside sprawl of gas stations, motels, and fast-food stands. But the old graveyard is kept in immaculate condition: it would be a credit to many a picturesque village with a white-painted church and a perfect row of maple trees.

Many of those buried here were killed in a succession of Indian raids. The most famous stone, near the center in a row of very old ones, marks the grave of Mr. Thomas Lund (d. 1724) :

> this Man with Seven
> more, that lies in this
> Grave; was Slew, All in
> A day, by the Indiens.

NEW BOSTON

New Boston Cemetery. [204] Drive uphill behind the town hall; as you approach the top, keep bearing to the right. The cemetery is alongside this road.

This peaceful hilltop cemetery is renowned for one gravestone of somewhat lurid interest. Approximately fifty feet behind the white building by the side of the road, a plain marble tablet marks the grave of Sevilla Jones, "Murdered by Henry N. Sargent Jan. 13, 1854, AEt. 17 yrs. 9 mos."

> Thus fell this lovely blooming daughter,
> By the revengeful hand—a malicious Henry,
> When on her way to school he met her,
> And with a six self cocked pistol shot her.

The epitaph is hard to believe but demonstrably genuine.

NEW CASTLE

Old Burying Ground. [205]   In the village center opposite the Congregational Church.

Very small, but choice. Notice the peculiar stone, in excellent condition, of Mrs. Abigail Frost (d. 1742). The key words of her verse epitaph are illustrated above it, in a curious symbolic tableau.

NEWMARKET

Joy Cemetery. [206]   On Packer Falls Road, which bears off to the right from Main Street, heading west from the village center. The road passes a large cemetery before coming to this one.

At the back of this small cemetery stands a granite monument to a grudge. On reflection, it is perhaps surprising that such monuments are not more common.

To the left is a huge monument in two colors of polished granite, erected in memory of Sarah E. Griffiths (d. 1887): its size and ostentation would be more appropriate in Mount Auburn than in a modest country graveyard. Apparently the executor of Mrs. Griffiths' estate spent more money on this monument than was to the liking of Mrs. Griffiths' heirs. And the monument, it appears, is rather more than that lady asked for in her will. To the right of the monument is a large piece of granite, engraved with a hand pointing at the Griffiths monument and the relevant extract from Sarah Griffiths' instructions: " 'A suitable monument and fit up the lot.'— S.E.G." The disappointed relative who took his revenge in this fashion did not append his own name; but the remainder of the inscription makes pointed reference to the fact that the

172

Erected
In memory of
Mr. JOHN SCOTT,
who departed this life 6
June 1798 Et. 90 years.

He was a native of Ireland
He was an honest man a
virtuous citizen and a good
member of society.

PETERBOROUGH

Joy and not the Griffiths family established this little cemetery in the first place. Indeed the entire front half of the lot is occupied by a kind of burial mound dedicated to the Joy family, which is in its own way rather strange.

PETERBOROUGH

 Old Town Cemetery. [207]   On Old Street Road, some distance east of the present village. To get to Old Street Road, drive east from the village on Route 101; turn north at the blinker light where Route 123 turns south. The cemetery is one mile north of Route 101.

The old cemetery on East Hill in Peterborough lies near the site of the town's first meeting house. The very first burying ground was next to the meeting house, further up the hill; but as this site proved impossibly rocky it was quickly abandoned. In former times, the Old Town Cemetery was carefully preserved: in 1908 the town published a book of gravestone inscriptions (still available from the Peterborough Historical Society) which is a model of its kind, and a series of numbered granite posts was placed around the periphery to facilitate the accurate location of every gravestone. Today the cemetery lies neglected and overgrown with weeds.

A plaque by the gate lists the names of thirty-nine Revolutionary soldiers buried within. There are a number of very interesting stones from the late eighteenth century. Fairly close together, toward the northern side, are the beautiful stones of Deacon Robert Smith (d. 1795) and Mr. John Scott (d. 1798), showing the human soul above an hourglass. Here and elsewhere, the tiny faces representing the soul are very delicately carved.

174

PORTSMOUTH

Old North Burial Ground. [208]   On Maplewood Avenue, west of the city center.

The largest of the old cemeteries in Portsmouth, and very crowded: contains a large number of substantial slates of the late eighteenth and early nineteenth centuries. Prominent tombs mark the graves of the Hon. William Whipple and Governor John Langdon, both signers of the Declaration of Independence. As examples of beautiful carving note the adjacent stones of Jacob and Hannah Sheafe, done in a modified portrait style which represents the Sheafes as angels. The huge slate stone of John Hale (d. 1796 ae. 33) bears a long and grandiloquent epitaph which concludes

> Long shall his Country, oft by f ction torn,
> Their faithful patriot, promis'd Father mourn;
> Nor to their splendid roll of Worthies fail
> To add with undissembled boast, an *HALE*.

Next to the Old North Burying Ground, with the effect of an addition, is Union Cemetery, containing grander monuments from the mid-nineteenth century.

Point of Graves. [209]   Mechanic Street, by the river: the approach is via Marcy Street (Route 1B), through a restored historic area.

The land known as Point of Graves was deeded to the town of Portsmouth in 1671, though at that time there had been burials there already. It stands today as an exceptionally fine (though small) collection of early slate stones, the earliest legible ones dating from the 1690's. A chart placed by the entrance indicates the work of various stonecutters represented here.

St. John's Churchyard. [210] Near the river on Chapel Street, behind City Hall.

To reach the churchyard, walk down along the right-hand side of the church and go around the back. Here are good slates in a distinguished setting, next to the very handsome brick church. The stone of Mrs. Elizabeth Turner, dated 1790, bears an unusually early example of the urn-and-willow design; it is a far more attractive carving than was customary in later years, when that design became universally popular. In the front row is a marble stone, unfortunately very hard to read, in memory of "the sensible warm motion of James Brackett Parrott, born Nov. 26, 1817, chilled by death Jan. 29, 1890. . . ."

St. John's Church itself should certainly be visited, for the graves of people buried within and for its own sake. Displayed inside is a copy of the rare "Vinegar Bible." This famous edition, printed at Oxford in 1717, gives "The Parable of the Vinegar" as a chapter-heading for Luke xx.

SALEM

 Salem Center Graveyard. [211] On Main Street (Route 97) at the town green: this is east of the central business district.

A small, attractive cemetery, set about with several handsome tamarack trees. Near the western corner note the long, glowing testimonial to the virtues of Harriet (d. 1815 ae. 19), second daughter of the Hon. Silas Betton.

TEMPLE

Village Cemetery. [212]   At the south end of the village green.

Small and secluded, offering a pleasant view of the valley to the east; it contains several fine eighteenth-century stones. Most impressive is the large portrait stone of the Rev. Samuel Webster (d. 1777), who "is doubtless rejoicing above, while thousands are mourning here below over his Grave!"

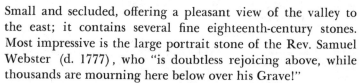

WALPOLE

Village Cemetery. [213]   On Turnpike Street, north of the center, opposite Walpole School.

What began as a small village burying ground has become a large cemetery. The old slates marking the graves of the original settlers can be found at the top of the hill, where there is a fine view of the Connecticut River valley.

Two large monuments, erected in the nineteenth century, stand in memory of two of the earliest settlers. They also commemorate a feud that grew up between the families of the two men. Near the front gate is a large granite monument to John Kilburn; up the hill behind it is a marble monument to Col. Benjamin Bellows. Each monument was erected by the man's descendants; each suggests plainly the man it names was the rightful founder of Walpole. Both men, in fact, had fought off the Indians to establish a settlement here, and both received charters to found a town. Kilburn received a charter in 1749—but his was a charter from New York State, which exercised no effective authority over the district. Soon Governor Wentworth of New Hampshire began to issue the "New Hampshire

Grants" establishing towns on both sides of the Connecticut River;
Col. Bellows received one of these in 1752. In the event, a New
Hampshire charter proved to be more potent than one from New
York, and Kilburn saw himself supplanted as founder. Although
both families remained in Walpole, it is said that they did not inter-
marry for 150 years.

WASHINGTON

Old Burying Ground. [214] Turn west (downhill) from
Route 31 at the bandstand in the village.

A peaceful, pleasant graveyard dating mostly from the nineteenth century. The star attraction is a small slate stone near
the road, inscribed "Capt. Samuel Jones' Leg which was
amputated July 7, 1804."

Seventh-Day Adventists Churchyard. [215] Begin with a visit
to the Old Burying Ground (see above); continue on the
same road for two miles, turning left on a dirt road. There is
a small sign marked "S.D.A. Church."

The first Seventh-Day Adventist congregation was formed in
this plain, white church building in 1862. A plaque nearby
gives an account of the developments that led to its formation.
The small churchyard could not be recommended without this
historical association, but it has a charming setting, surrounded by woods, and is carefully maintained.

RHODE ISLAND

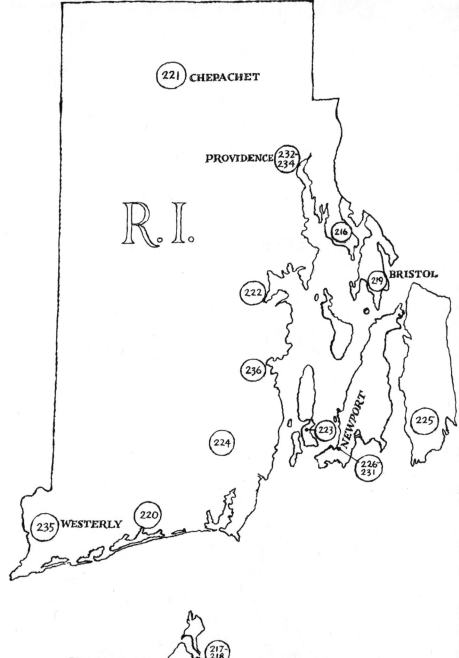

216. Barrington
217, 218. Block Island
219. Bristol
220. Charlestown
221. Chepachet
222. East Greenwich
223. Jamestown

224. Kingston
225. Little Compton
226–231. Newport
232–234. Providence
235. Westerly
236. Wickford

NEWPORT

*No Church-yard is so handsome,
that a man would desire straight
to be buried there.*

GEORGE HERBERT

*The country home I need is a
cemetery.*

MARK TWAIN (C. 1900)

BARRINGTON

Tyler Point Burying Ground. [216]   On Tyler Point Road, which runs west from Route 114, at a point just north of the Barrington/Warren town line.

The first burying ground in Barrington, established in 1702. It is pleasantly situated on a point of land by the small-boat harbor. Among the older gravestones, note the fine portrait stone of Capt. John Kelley (d. 1777).

BLOCK ISLAND

Block Island Cemetery. [217]   On West Side Road, a short distance west of the dock at New Harbor; on a hill above the road.

The largest, most attractive, and most easily accessible of the cemeteries on Block Island: the others tend to be small family cemeteries, difficult to find. A driveway divides the grounds into old and new sections. The older section, well maintained, contains graves of early settlers and Revolutionary soldiers.

Palatine Cemetery. [218]   Near the Dickens homestead, off Cooneymus Road. Drive westward along Cooneymus Road; just before the road ends, at Warden's Pond, take the left-hand turn onto Dickens Road. Follow this road to a small white house. The Palatine monument is visible from this point.

The Palatine Cemetery, once comprising small clusters of graves, is now marked by just a single monument. Here were buried the survivors of the *Palatine* shipwreck—for most of them survived only briefly.

About 1720, a Dutch ship left Rotterdam filled with emigrants bound for New York and Pennsylvania. The name of the ship has been long forgotten, but it is traditionally called the *Palatine:* its passengers were themselves called "Palatines," emigrants from the Rhineland-Palatinate area of Germany. All accounts relate that it was a disastrous passage, though the details vary a great deal. According to the most vivid story, the voyage was originally delayed by winter storms. Diminished supplies and consequent hardships led to a mutiny and the murder of the captain; the rebellious crew then seized such supplies as remained and auctioned them off to the starving passengers. Eventually the crew deserted the ship and left her adrift. When the Palatine ship finally ran aground on Sandy Point, the Block Islanders rescued sixteen survivors; one woman of great wealth, who had gone mad, refused to abandon her possessions and leave the ship. A storm arose, and to prevent the *Palatine* from breaking up on the shore the rescuers fired the ship and cut her adrift once more. Suddenly they were petrified by the screams of the mad woman, trapped aboard the burning ship, who had been forgotten in the excitement.

Those who find some of the details of that story unlikely may prefer the second, more straightforward version. According to some sources, the *Palatine* was lured onto the rocks by wreckers, who then fired the ship to conceal their abominable crime. (That the passengers were either dead or on the point of starvation is accepted by all authorities.) This latter version is the one adopted by John Greenleaf Whittier in "The Palatine," a poem from *The Tent on the Beach.*

> . . . Into the teeth of death she sped:
> (May God forgive the hands that fed
> The false lights over the rocky Head!)
>
> O men and brothers! what sights were there!
> White upturned faces, hands stretched in prayer!
> Where waves had pity, could ye not spare?
>
> Down swooped the wreckers like birds of prey
> Tearing the heart of the ship away,
> And the dead had never a word to say. . . .

There have been persistent allegations over the years that the old Cornish practice of wrecking did indeed flourish for a time on Block Island. The Islanders are sensitive on the subject, but it may be observed that they refer to wreckers by a familiar euphemism or nickname: the wreckers are called "mooncussers," since of course on a moonlit night no ship can be lured unwittingly onto the rocks.

For over a hundred years after the shipwreck, a phenomenon known as the Palatine Light was observed over the ocean off the northern part of Block Island. This strange illumination, attested to by reputable observers, was said by many to resemble the image of the blazing ship as it drifted out to sea. Dr. Aaron Willey, a physician on the Island, described the phenomenon in a letter to a colleague, written in 1811: "Its appearance is nothing different from a blaze of fire; whether it actually touches the water, or merely hovers over it, is uncertain, for I am informed that no person has been near enough to decide accurately. It beams with various magnitudes, and appears to bear no more analogy to the *ignis fatuus* than it does to the aurora borealis. Sometimes it is small, resembling the light through a distant window; at others expanding to the highness of a ship with all her canvass spread. When large, it displays either a pyramidical form, or three constant streams. In the latter case, the streams are somewhat blended together at the bottom, but separate and distinct at the top, while the middle one rises rather higher than the other two. . . ."

BRISTOL

 East Burial Ground. [219]   On Wood Street, near the town center. Wood Street runs parallel to Route 114, two blocks to the east.

A large graveyard, with signs of crowding in earlier times; it was established in 1739 and was Bristol's chief burying place into the nineteenth century. Today it is unkempt, overgrown, its stones broken and toppled. Nevertheless there remain interesting stones which are worth examining. One such is the marker of "Two Promising Sons of Mr. Stephen Wardwell," d. 1796, decorated at the top with a pair of anchors. The really famous gravestone here can be found fairly easily, near the fence in the southwest corner. This stone, for Mrs. Sarah Swan (d. 1767), shows Adam and Eve in the Garden of Eden, the tree and the snake between them.

CHARLESTOWN

Indian Royal Burying Ground. [220] From Route 1, drive 1¼ miles north on State Route 2; then ¾ mile east on Narrow Lane to the burying ground entrance. The burying ground is reached on foot, by an uphill path.

The Charlestown Indian Burying Ground is less a cemetery than a historic site. The only visible monument is one "erected by the State of Rhode Island, to mark the place which Indian tradition identifies as the Royal Burying Ground of the Narragansett Tribe, and in recognition of the kindness and hospitality of this once-powerful Nation to the founders of this State." Otherwise this is simply a fenced-off rectangle of mossy ground; it would be completely isolated were it not for the noise of distant highway traffic which penetrates the forest.

So this graveyard can hardly be recommended to those whose sole interest is gravestones and monuments. Nevertheless a visit may be worthwhile, for this burying ground, such as it is, is one of the few visible indications that "New England" was home to another civilization long before the Pilgrims landed.

Those who are interested in the Indians of New England may wish to visit the Narragansett Indian Church nearby. To get there, return to Route 2 and continue one mile further north. Turn left as indicated by a sign, then left again at another sign, and continue along a gravel road approximately ½ mile to the church driveway. The church was built in 1859 and is still in use. In back is a small graveyard with crudely marked stones.

CHEPACHET

Chepachet Cemetery. [221] On Route 44, at the southern edge of the village.

Chepachet Cemetery would be of no particular interest apart from its site. The cemetery occupies Acote Hill in Chepachet, and on Acote Hill took place the climactic scene of a remarkable and little-known episode of American history. At the foot of the hill, next to the road, is a monument to Thomas W. Dorr (1805–54), leader of the "Dorr War" of 1842 and, for a time, the outlaw governor of Rhode Island. The monument reads, "Framer of the People's Constitution of 1842 . . . Elected Governor under it . . . Adjudged revolutionary 1842 . . . Principles acknowledged right 1912." The monument was, in fact, erected in the enlightened year of 1912. (Dorr himself is buried at Swan Point, Providence: see below.)

In the year 1842 Rhode Island was still being governed under its Royal Charter of 1663. This antiquated document, among its other provisions, disqualified from suffrage fully half the adult male population by means of property requirements. After the failure of numerous attempts at reform, Dorr founded a People's Party which called an extra-legal constitutional convention; the People's Party then held a referendum in which the People's Constitution was ratified. In May, 1842, Dorr was elected governor under the new constitution. At this point Rhode Island had two governors and two

NEWPORT

governments. The established government, under Governor Samuel King, began to arrest Dorr's followers. Planning his resistance, Dorr arranged to meet in Chepachet with five hundred armed supporters: only fifty appeared, and Dorr withdrew. Thereupon took place the one battle of the Dorr War. Governor King, to demonstrate his mastery of the field, sent his regulars to storm Acote Hill. One cow was killed in the skirmish. Dorr was imprisoned for one year. The final victory was his, however, as a legitimate constitutional convention met later in 1842 to draw up the modern State Constitution of Rhode Island.

EAST GREENWICH

Old Baptist Burial Ground. [222]   At the end of Wine Street. Wine Street runs eastward from Main Street (Route 1), but does not come through onto Main Street. It lies in between King and Division Streets, and may be reached via either of these streets.

A small graveyard, half-forgotten, hard to find; and it must be admitted, there is not a great deal to see when you get there. But it is a pleasant, secluded spot, and there is a certain pleasure in visiting a cemetery which lies in the center of the village but is unknown to most residents.

The modest grounds are well kept. There remain only a handful of stones, but among these are some beautiful items. In the far corner, overgrown with honeysuckle, is an interesting stone for Mr. Russel Greene, "who was drowned in passing Narragansett Ferry . . . (1768) — His Body was not found."

J A M E S T O W N

Old Friends' Burial Ground. [223] On Eldred Avenue
(Route 138), ½ mile west of North Main Road. The more
recent Cedar Cemetery is adjacent to the east.

This small plot surrounded by a stone wall is a relic of the
days when Jamestown had a large Quaker population. It contains the graves of many early settlers and Revolutionary
soldiers. Most interesting among these is the grave of Capt.
John Eldred, d. 1784 ae. 72.

During the Revolutionary War Eldred set up his famous One-Gun
Battery on the eastern side of Coanicut Island and took potshots at
British vessels sailing into Narragansett Bay. Eldred managed to
make such a nuisance of his one cannon that the British sent a land-
ing party to silence what they presumed was an artillery company.
They found Eldred's gun and spiked it.

Stepping-stones set into the wall at the back lead to the even
smaller cemetery of the Hazard family, interesting not so much
for its stones as for its charming size and setting.

K I N G S T O N

"The Platform." [224] In the Town of North Kingstown, on
Shermantown Road, ⅞ mile west of combined Routes 1 and
138. Access to the cemetery is by a grassy lane through the
woods: the start of the lane is marked by a sign on the south
side of Shermantown Road.

The cemetery known today as "The Platform" was originally
the churchyard of St. Paul's Church, on this site. St. Paul's
was erected here in 1707; in 1800 it was moved to Wickford
(see below), a distance of some 5½ miles, in the space of a

week. It left behind an isolated, though not an abandoned, cemetery: burials continued here into the 1880's. There remains today an interesting assortment of old stones in a partially walled, charmingly secluded setting.

LITTLE COMPTON

Old Burying Ground. [225]   In Little Compton Commons, at the center of the village.

An attractive old cemetery with some exceptionally interesting stones. A table stone marks the grave of Benjamin Church (1639–1718), a famous Indian fighter in King Philip's War. Church was a leader of the colonial forces in the Great Swamp Fight (1675) and was responsible for Philip's death the following year. Elisabeth Pabodie, the daughter of John and Priscilla Alden, is buried beneath a granite obelisk containing her original gravestone; the more recent monument recognizes her as the first white woman born in New England.

Even more famous are the stones of Mr. Simeon Palmer's wives. They are among the Palmer family graves, toward the north side of the cemetery, on a line from the Pabodie monument to the town hall. Here lie "Lidia the Wife of Mr. Simeon Palmer," d. 1754 ae. 35, and "Elizabeth who Should have been the Wife of Mr. Simeon Palmer," d. 1776 ae. 64. A tale of remorse and of unrequited love—no doubt. But its precise interpretation is changed somewhat by the fact that, according to town records, Elizabeth *was* legally wedded to Mr. Palmer after Lidia's death.

NEWPORT

Arnold Burying Ground. [226]   Beside the house at 70 Pelham Street.

The Arnold family cemetery, established in 1677, was a model restoration project of twenty-five years ago. It contains a small but unusually fine collection of seventeenth-century stones. Buried here is Governor Benedict Arnold—not the traitorous general, but the man who served as colonial governor of Rhode Island in the 1660's and 70's.

Common Burying Ground. [227]   On Farewell Street, at the corner of Warner Street.

The large and crowded Common Burying Ground in Newport has one of the best collections of fine eighteenth-century stonecutting to be found in New England. The land was given to the City of Newport in 1640, originally as a burial place for strangers. It contains today some three thousand stones and an unknown number of graves.

The impressive older section lies up the hill from the entrance, toward the Island Cemetery which lies on the other side of the fence. The riches of artistry and design to be found here are in large part due to the work of four men: a grandfather, father, and son all named John Stevens, and one John Bull. All these men worked in Newport; John Stevens III and John Bull were contemporaries and customarily signed their work. The two most spectacular single pieces are thus readily identified as the work of John Bull. One is a multiple headstone for the six sons and daughters of William Langley, all of whom died in infancy between 1771 and 1785: it is easily found in the high grass because of its great horizontal length. The other, near the central path up the hill, is the stone of

Charles Bardin (d. 1773) : it bears the only direct representation of God on a gravestone in New England. God is shown amid the clouds, with arms outstretched, in an approximate imitation of Michelangelo's Sistine Chapel ceiling. Also in this vicinity is an undecorated slate stone inscribed as follows: "The human form respected for its honesty, and known 53 years by the appellation CHRISTOPHER ELLERY, began to dissolve in the month of February 1789."

Near the entrance, with an emblem of an anchor crossed with oars, is a granite memorial to Ida Lewis (d. 1911), "the grace darling of America / Keeper of Lime Rock Lighthouse / Newport Harbor / Erected by her many kind friends." At the north end of the cemetery, under the cherry trees, are the graves of eighteenth-century Negro slaves. The slate markers are somewhat smaller than usual; several are beautifully carved.

Governors' Graveyard. [228]　On Farewell Street, opposite Mumford School.

A small, shallow plot which nevertheless contains the graves of seven of Rhode Island's colonial governors. There is just enough here to invite a brief stop.

Island Cemetery. [229]　On Warner Street, adjacent to the Common Burying Ground.

On the other side of the fence from the Common Burying Ground lies, as cemeteries go, another world. The Island Cemetery is a grand nineteenth-century foundation containing heroes' graves and splendid monuments.

The two great heroes are of course the brothers Oliver Hazard Perry (1785–1819) and Matthew Calbraith Perry (1794–1858). Commodore Oliver Perry was the victor of the

WESTERLY

Battle of Lake Erie on September 10, 1813; it was after this victory that he informed General William H. Harrison, "We have met the enemy and they are ours." He died of yellow fever in Port of Spain, Trinidad and was originally buried there. A few years later, after a Congressional Resolution, his body was returned to Newport and reinterred in Island Cemetery. Commodore Matthew Perry spent the War of 1812 blockaded by the British in New London harbor. His days of glory came in 1853–54 when he presided over the "opening" of Japan: a carefully orchestrated display of naval strength led to the conclusion of a treaty opening two Japanese ports to American trade under improved conditions.

Another naval monument stands by the grave of Capt. Mathias Marin (d. 1895) : it consists of a huge stone book next to an immense marble anchor. Further down the drive is the large and elaborate tomb of August Belmont (1816–90), one of the legendary leaders of New York and Newport society. It is surrounded by lesser graves of the Belmont and Perry families: Belmont's social position was cemented by his marriage to the daughter of Matthew Perry. A short distance away, the seated bronze figure of August Belmont regards the scene, holding his chin with a pensive, paterfamilias expression. The most striking of all the monuments in Island Cemetery is a pre-Raphaelite angel in faded pink marble at the tomb of Annamaria Smith, executed by Augustus Saint-Gaudens in 1886.

The Jewish Cemetery. [230]   Head of Touro Street, at Bellevue Avenue. Kept locked, unfortunately. Most of it can be seen from outside the fence.

Newport had one of the first Jewish colonies in America when fifteen families of Jews arrived from Holland in 1658. The

land for this small cemetery was purchased in 1677; the earliest
stones remaining date from the eighteenth century. The cemetery is very well kept and most attractive. The stones are inscribed in numerous languages, reflecting the varied origins of
Newport's Jewish settlers; here one can admire the extraordinary sight of an eighteenth-century slate stone, decorated
with an angel in the most classical New England style, inscribed with Hebrew characters. There is a poem by Longfellow entitled, "The Jewish Cemetery at Newport."

How strange it seems! These Hebrews in their graves,
  Close by the street of this fair seaport town,
Silent beside the never-silent waves,
  At rest in all this moving up and down!

.   .   .   .

The very names recorded here are strange,
  Of Foreign accent, and of different climes;
Alvares and Rivera interchange
  With Abraham and Jacob of old times.

Trinity Churchyard. [231] At the corner of Church and
Spring Streets.

In any town lacking Newport's wealth of cemeteries, the fine
stones of this churchyard would make it better known. There
is a large number of ledger stones, laid flat in the ground, as
is more common with burials inside churches; many of these
are beautifully carved. Note the adjacent stones of John
Gidley, his son, and their respective wives: the son died in
1744, ae. 44, "having received the fated Citation for Death by
a violent Explosion of Gun-Powder eleven Days before He
Expired." Most elaborate of all is the spendid stone in the
southeast corner, "Erected by George Gibbs, Merchant" for his
Amiable Consort, Susannah, d. 1767 ae. 22.

PROVIDENCE

North Burial Ground. [232] On North Main Street at Branch Avenue.

The oldest public cemetery in Providence; established in 1700 for "a training field, burying ground, and other public uses." There is a great variety of monuments, increased by the fact that groups of older stones were moved here from small cemeteries during the nineteenth century.

The older stones are found near the main entrance. Some of the most interesting mark the graves of the Brown family. It was Nicholas Brown (d. 1841) in honor of whose philanthropies the former Rhode Island College was renamed Brown University. The most imposing of these stones was put up as a memorial to his ancestor, Chad Brown: it bears an unusual heart-shaped carving. Some distance away, a pair of slates (recognizable by their curious pointed shape) mark the graves of Charles and Lucy Haskell, Negro servants; the stones were evidently erected by their wealthy employer. Charles Haskell's stone describes him as "a man of colour" and a Revolutionary soldier; his wife's stone carries a punning epitaph on her color.

Grander creations, easily visible, include a magnificent bronze elk for the fraternal plot and a fine statue of a fireman on the Providence Fire Department monument.

St. John's Churchyard. [233] Behind St. John's Episcopal Church, North Main Street.

The small but interesting collection of old stones is worth a brief visit. Those buried here comprised a good part of Providence aristocracy in the eighteenth century.

Swan Point Cemetery. [234]   North of the city center on
Blackstone Boulevard.

A large and handsome cemetery laid out in the grand manner
of the nineteenth century. The monuments at Swan Point are
not, on the whole, as extravagant as those at Mount Auburn;
but the grounds are even larger (210 acres), and they are landscaped and maintained with equal care. The cemetery enjoys
a striking situation above the Seekonk River. It is planted with
255 different varieties of trees and shrubs, all identified and
labelled. At last count, there were twenty-three governors of
Rhode Island buried at Swan Point, including the "anti-
Governor" of the Great Schism of 1842, Thomas W. Dorr.
(There is a monument to Dorr at Chepachet: see above.)

One of the more interesting monuments stands on the lot
of the Sayles family. Within a miniature temple of mixed
classical style is the bronze figure of a young man, reading a
book: this scion of the Sayles family died while a student at
Brown University. The Sprague lot, a large oval, is filled with
evergreen plantings and contains no stones at all. Amasa
Sprague, whose name is inscribed, was the brother of one governor of Rhode Island and father of another.

Somewhat difficult to find, since the name is inscribed on the
monument of another family, is the grave of H. P. Lovecraft
(1890–1937). (Cultists may ask directions at the cemetery
office.) Lovecraft, author of novels and short stories, was an
acknowledged master of the gothic horror story and a pioneer
in the art of science fiction. Most of his stories appeared in the
magazine *Weird Tales,* where they reached an enthusiastic
although limited audience. Since his death, and particularly
in recent years, Lovecraft's work has become much more
widely admired.

WESTERLY

River Bend Cemetery. [235]   On Beach Street (Route 1A), 1½ miles south of the city center.

An attractive setting along the Pawcatuck River; swans nest on the riverbank and may be seen swimming back and forth. The graves are primarily modern, but there are a number of interesting monuments carved of the local Westerly granite. One of the less obvious, but most interesting, of these is the dark gray granite memorial bearing a relief bust of Stanton Clark, 1820–19– (with the date of death never filled in).

WICKFORD

Old St. Paul's Churchyard. [236]   To visit Old St. Paul's as one is intended to do, follow the pathway that begins just east of St. Paul's Parish House at 76 Main Street.

The little churchyard of Old St. Paul's, also known as the Old Narragansett Church, can hardly be recommended for the sake of its stones. But a visit to this attractive church building in its Wickford setting is necessary to complete the story which begins at "The Platform" near Kingston (see above). The flagstones along the pathway give the history of this moveable church and the dates of service of all its rectors.

VERMONT

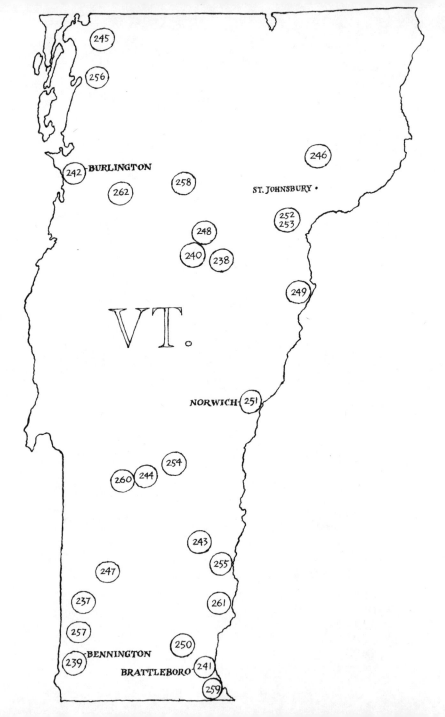

237. Arlington
238. Barre
239. Bennington
240. Berlin Corners
241. Brattleboro
242. Burlington
243. Chester
244. Cuttingsville
245. Highgate Center
246. Lyndon Center
247. Manchester
248. Montpelier
249. Newbury

250. Newfane
251. Norwich
252, 253. Peacham
254. Plymouth
255. Rockingham
256. St. Albans
257. Shaftsbury Center
258. Stowe
259. Vernon
260. Wallingford
261. Westminster
262. Williston

No man who needs a monument
ever ought to have one.

NATHANIEL HAWTHORNE

PEACHAM

A R L I N G T O N

St. James's Churchyard. [237]   Next to St. James Episcopal Church, on Route 7.

A crowded old churchyard enclosed by a neat stone wall. The present church, a handsome gray stone building, was erected in 1830. One of those buried here is Mary Brownson, the first wife of Ethan Allen.

Among an attractive assortment of stones, the most interesting are the examples of eighteenth-century work in marble. Such stones are something of a rarity in any case; among the examples at Arlington is one that is downright peculiar. This is a small stone, directly in front of the gateway, at the grave of Miriam Hawley (d. 1796). It bears an amusing, cartoon-like portrait: the face a perfect circle, wavy hair in symmetrical spirals. There are large, handsomely cut marble stones from the nineteenth century as well.

B A R R E

Hope Cemetery. [238]   On Maple Avenue (Route 14), north of Route 302.

Hope Cemetery, as a whole, stands as a monument to Barre's famous granite quarries and to the men who came here to work in them. To begin with, every monument in Hope Cemetery is made of the local granite: this includes the elaborate sculptures that, anywhere else, would have been done in marble. The unaccustomed sight of row upon row of the largest, most elaborate modern granite markers tends to suggest a display outside a rather expensive monument works.

What is more interesting is the people. Barre began with a predominantly Scotch population, whose monument might be said to be the Robert Burns statue which stands above City Park. But skilled stone carvers for the granite works came increasingly from Italy, and Italian names outnumber all others on the monuments in Hope Cemetery. Most of the monuments were designed by these artisans for themselves and for members of their families.

In this collection of exceptional monuments, some are particularly impressive. One of the monuments of the Brusa family includes an agreeably casual angel, seated with her legs crossed in a rather tomboyish manner. The startling tomb of William and Gwendolyn Halvosa includes a large double portrait stone placed in such a way as to give the impression that they are sitting up beside each other in a double bed. In a newer section of somewhat smaller monuments, note the stone of Albert Ceppi, which depicts him at work on an engraving of Christ; beneath is the legend, *Scultore Supremo*.

Most interesting of all is the large monument to Elia Corti (d. 1903). Corti is shown life-size, seated on a projecting ledge from a cliff of granite. He appears to be dressed for a Sunday afternoon of *dolce far niente* at an elegant, turn-of-the-century café, but his face bears a meditative expression. Corti was a distinguished stonecutter whose work included the panels at the base of the Burns statue; in 1903, as an innocent bystander at a riot provoked by local anarchists, he was shot to death. The splendid monument was designed and produced as a tribute by his fellow craftsmen.

BENNINGTON

Old Bennington Cemetery. [239] In Old Bennington, one mile west of the present town center on Route 9.

This particularly lovely cemetery, beside the First Church (Congregationalist) on Old Bennington Green, forms part of one of the classic settings of Old New England. Among the Revolutionary soldiers buried here are both British and American dead from the Battle of Bennington (August 1777), in which the Green Mountain Boys under John Stark and Seth Warner defeated the Hessian mercenaries of General Burgoyne. Five Vermont governors are buried here, including the brilliant Federalist statesman Isaac Tichenor (1754–1838). Most noteworthy of all is the grave of the poet Robert Frost (1874–1963), lying toward the back of the cemetery. It bears the epitaph, "I had a lover's quarrel with the world."

A number of the markers from the late eighteenth century display an intricacy of carving comparatively unusual in marble gravestones.

BERLIN CORNERS

Berlin Corners Cemetery. [240] Just south of the Berlin First Congregational Church.

A modest cemetery, lying behind an iron fence and a row of handsome maple trees. Near the road is one stone which is famous. Hosea B. Foster, d. 1859 ae. 21, is depicted wearing a dress suit and reading a Bible while an angel behind him lifts him off to heaven. In the same row of stones, Miss Emma Adelaide Vaughn (d. 1857 ae. 15) is also shown being carried off by an angel; the favorable reception accorded this stone

BARRE

doubtless prompted the more elaborate Foster commission, two years later. Other agreeable nineteenth-century markers include many excellent pointing fingers.

BRATTLEBORO

Prospect Hill Cemetery. [241]   South Main Street.

On the southern edge of this hilltop cemetery—most of which is comprised of fairly commonplace nineteenth-century stones —is a curved ridge affording a splendid view into the valley of the Connecticut River below. Here, not surprisingly, are the grander monuments and the graves of Brattleboro's wealthiest families in former times. And here, most surprisingly, is the glorious and audacious tomb of Col. James Fisk (1834–72), renowned playboy and Robber Baron, the victim of one of the most sensational love-triangle murders in the history of New York City. Fisk's monument, set up in this quiet corner of the well-mannered State of Vermont, is adorned at its corners by four marble females of obvious charms and doubtful modesty. Unclothed above the waist, they hold in their laps the tokens of Fisk's lost empire: one, a large volume entitled "Railroads"; another, "Steamboats"; a third, succinctly, holds a large sack of coins. The temptations posed by this work of art have at times been too much for passersby, and the lovelies are sadly missing numerous fingers, a foot, a nose. . . . The monument remains a three-star masterpiece.

"Jubilee Jim" Fisk, born in the tiny hamlet of North Pownal, Vermont, made as big a splash in the outside world as Ethan Allen and rather more of one than did Calvin Coolidge. As a youth he worked in a circus; later he set himself up in business as a Yankee peddler, traveling the country with a wagon full of merchandise. During the Civil War Fisk made a fortune by means which an unfriendly observer might call "profiteering"—buying cotton in occupied areas of the South for Northern brokers and selling worthless Confederate bonds in England. After the War he established a Wall Street brokerage house with the notorious Daniel Drew: Fisk, Drew, and Jay Gould then engaged in a famous and successful battle with Cornelius Vanderbilt for control of the Erie Railroad, a battle which at times included the armed conflict of mercenaries for physical control of the tracks. Fisk and Gould, then styled "Prince of Erie," used their control to engage in stock manipulations which gained them millions and ruined the railroad. Their most famous financial exploit, however, was a nearly successful attempt to corner the gold market. The resulting panic ruined thousands of speculators on September 24, 1869—the original "Black Friday."

Fisk had meanwhile gained the popular fancy by his reputation as a reckless gambler and by such caprices as his purchase of an opera house in which to show off his doxy of the moment. His career came suddenly to its premature and spectacular finish. As Fisk was descending the stairway into the lobby of the elegant Broadway Central Hotel in New York he was shot dead by Ed Stokes, a former business associate and his rival for the affections of the actress Josie Mansfield. Although the identity of the murderer was known to every man, woman, and child in New York, Stokes was never convicted of first degree murder and was consequently never hanged. As any well-connected (and guilty) defendant would have done at the time, Stokes retained the noted firm of Howe & Hummel, criminal lawyers, for his defense. Agents of the firm (according to Hummel, many years later) discovered that there was only one actual eyewitness to the shooting: they reached this man quickly and offered him a very large sum of money to leave the country and never return. He accepted. This turn of events, combined with their usual courtroom skill, enabled the partners to save the neck of Miss Mansfield's remaining admirer.

BURLINGTON

 Greenmount Cemetery. [242]   On Colchester Avenue, just south of the Winooski River Bridge.

The central, imposing feature of Greenmount Cemetery is the massive monument to Ethan Allen (1737–89). A forty-two foot granite shaft is surmounted by a statue of Allen eight feet high. Arms upraised, he is shown at the most famous moment of his career, as he demanded the surrender of Fort Ticonderoga "in the name of the Great Jehovah and the Continental Congress." Next to this is a small obelisk in memory of General Ira Allen (1751–1814). General Allen's remains, however, lie elsewhere.

Ira Allen is vaguely remembered today as a Vermont pioneer and Revolutionary patriot. There was a darker side to his career as well: the man has been called "the Metternich of Vermont." The founders of the State of Vermont fought two battles. One was their part in the American Revolution; the other was the struggle for recognition of Vermont as a separate state, safe from the conflicting claims of New Hampshire and New York. The Continental Congress was not quick to recognize Vermont's independence. Allen, then one of Vermont's principal negotiators with the Congress, tried another tack. In 1780 he was involved in secret discussions with representatives of the British about a possible separate peace for Vermont, by which the state would become a British province with British troops to guarantee its borders. The proposal seems to have been a serious one, but it became moot with the cessation of hostilities between England and America in 1783.

In 1789 Allen brought about the founding of the University of Vermont, making a £4000 gift for the purpose. In 1795 he was engaged in international arms dealing, buying munitions in France for the Vermont militia; his returning ship was seized by the British, who were then at war with the revolutionary government of France. When Allen finally returned to Burlington in 1801 he was imprisoned for debt. Released by the legislature, he left Vermont for Philadelphia, where he spent the last years of his life in poverty and obscurity. There he was buried in an unmarked grave in the old Free Quaker Cemetery on Fifth Street—long since obliterated.

CHESTER

Chester Cemetery. [243]   On Route 11, opposite the village green.

A pleasant village cemetery, fairly large and crowded: it is worth a brief visit. Among the old slates, dating from the 1780's, is an interesting series of angels with angular wings. Other stones show a small sun with a face.

CUTTINGSVILLE

Laurel Glen Cemetery. [244]   On Route 103, just south of the village.

The famous attraction of Laurel Glen Cemetery is hard to miss: it looms directly over the road. This is the large mausoleum erected by John P. Bowman, who formerly lived in the wooden mansion across the road. The mausoleum was built to hold the remains of Bowman's wife and two daughters, with space for Bowman himself at his death.

Kneeling on the front steps of the mausoleum is a granite figure of John P. Bowman, much larger than life. In his hands he holds his top hat, a wreath, and a key: his posture is one of supplication, awaiting the day when he may be allowed to join his family within the tomb. Such unmistakable emotion, seen in the features of an eight-foot granite man, is little short of overpowering. This astonishing sculpture is the work of G. Turini, N.Y., 1881.

The inner doors of the mausoleum are left open, revealing a tiled floor, walls of engraved marble, chairs, mirrors, busts of Bowman and his wife, and a sculpture of the infant daughter.

Both the interior and exterior of this monument are in excellent condition. One reason is that it is carefully closed up and covered during the winter months. Cuttingsville must therefore be a summertime destination.

HIGHGATE CENTER

 Center Cemetery. [245]   South of Route 78, behind the firehouse in the village.

In Highgate Center—and many villages like it—a good-sized local cemetery recalls the days when the town was a more populous and more prosperous place than it is now. The gravestones of several doctors, for instance, show that not so long ago Highgate Center had its own doctor, practicing full time in town. Today, the residents must travel over to Swanton or St. Albans. A few of the markers have a cherished local significance. Underneath the Colorado spruce in the middle of the cemetery (and there are men alive who remember the day when it was planted, brought in from Colorado) is a squat

CUTTINGSVILLE

marble pillar marking the grave of Mr. Goit. The name is pronounced in two syllables; and the inscription, barely legible, reads "I can't stay here." Not far away is another stone that is much prized: it stands above the grave of Emily A., wife of Henry Death. The modern monument nearby, in polished granite, has a story connected with it. Some people in town remember that the man buried beneath it—who lived to a ripe and honorable age—ran away from his army camp during the first World War and hid for several days in a big cave over toward Highgate Falls. It is clear that his troubles got straightened out somehow, for the grave is marked with an American Legion flagholder. Way over on the far side is the biggest monument of all, with a female figure sculptured in marble. The man it commemorates, Mr. Redding, was "summer people" from New York, back in the 1890's. People in Highgate Center figure that Mr. Redding has no family left these days, since they've never seen anyone put flowers at the grave.

LYNDON CENTER

 Lyndon Center Cemetery. [246]   Behind the Town House, on the village green.

An extensive, nineteenth-century cemetery, spread over a hillside. Midway up the central driveway is a large marble monument designed for himself by George P. Spencer (1825–1908), a stonecutter and a public atheist. On top of the monument is the disarming figure of a little babe, asleep with its head on a pillow: beneath this is the inscription, "A dreamless sleep, emblem of eternal rest." If Spencer had left it at that, he would have raised no eyebrows at all. But the rest of the monu-

ROCKINGHAM

ment is covered with a series of unambiguous slogans. "Science
has never killed or persecuted a single person for doubting or
denying its teachings, and most of these teachings have been
true: but religion has murdered millions for doubting or denying her dogmas, and most of these dogmas have been false."
"The lips of the dead are closed forever, there comes no voice
from the tomb." There are many more. Some of the inscriptions have been partially defaced—a fact which would
doubtless give Spencer a certain satisfaction, could he awake
from his dreamless sleep to observe it.

There is a likely-looking dog at the foot of the Mathewson
monument, along the same driveway.

MANCHESTER

Dellwood Cemetery. [247]   On Route 7 at the southern edge
of town.

On the east side of the brook which runs through Dellwood
Cemetery is one remarkable monument: a magnificent marble
angel, kneeling at the tomb of Arthur Taylor (d. 1900). The
older stones, near the entrance, are less striking but well worth
a look. Notice, in the second row, the curiously shaped stone
of Mrs. Desire B. Allis, the Amiable Consort of Doctor Abel
Allis, d. 1796 ae. 23. In the fourth row, the double headstone
of John and Susannah Roberts bears a noble epitaph:

> Princes, this clay must be your bead,
> In spite of all your powers;
> The Tall the Wise the Reverend Head,
> Must lie as low as ours.

MONTPELIER

Green Mount Cemetery. [248]   On State Street (Route 2), at the western edge of town.

A large cemetery in the grand style, with impressive monuments of local granite. The entrance is marked by a massive gate of all-purpose Renaissance design. The grounds stretch up a steep, terraced hillside providing a fine view from the top.

Visible from the entrance is the agreeable monument erected by the City of Montpelier to Joel Foster (1825–1903), for many years Superintendent of the Water Works. A statue of Mr. Foster shows him holding a derby hat and leaning on a fire hydrant. Somewhat further along is a very elaborate monument to John E. Hubbard, inscribed with a verse which —at this proximity to the great quarries of Vermont granite— seems peculiarly pointed: "Thou go not like the quarry slave at night, scourged to his dungeon. . . ." At the far eastern end of the cemetery is another Hubbard family monument, unusually ambitious, constructed of red granite with a bronze *pietà*. Also at this end, by the road, steps have been cut to form a memorial of a huge mass of protruding natural rock. Affixed to the hillside is a bronze plaque bearing an enlarged reproduction of the signature of W. A. Stowell, whose memorial this presumably is. The upper reaches of the cemetery contain a large number of fine angels.

NEWBURY

Oxbow Cemetery. [249]   On Route 5, north of the village.

A large cemetery, in continuous use from the 1770's to the present. It offers spectacular views down into the "Oxbow" of

219

the Connecticut River, and eastward to the mountains of New Hampshire.

The old stones of the early settlers may be found not far from the main entrance. Among the newer monuments, a marble obelisk marks the grave of Clark T. Hinman, D.C., the Methodist founder and first president of Northwestern University (d. 1854 ae. 35). Further along is an unusually large marble tree trunk, including a marble wreath, marble drapery, and a marble bird, all in memory of Col. Thomas Johnson (d. 1819). The monument was, of course, erected many years later by the Colonel's descendants.

The most interesting monument of all is a white marble tablet, not far from the tree trunk and next to a small obelisk. This remarkable stone is in memory of Harriet Ruggles Loomis, the wife of a West African missionary. She was born in Newbury in 1824; she died at "Corisco, W.A." in 1861—or, more precisely, at 55' N., 9° 17' 30" E. (Corisco is an island off the coast of Rio Muni in Equatorial Guinea.)

A beautiful engraving shows the tiny harbor at Corisco, a ship arriving, the neat rows of huts beneath the palm trees. Beneath the picture are Mrs. Loomis's parting words: "I never regretted coming to Africa; ten years I prayed for this privilege; the bitterness of death is not bitter; don't grieve for me; it is all right." At the very bottom of the stone is a hand pointing upward and this further inscription:

> Ebe bobe ome, Ebe njuke na ngebe
> O yenek'o buhua; O ka bange vake.

NEWFANE

Newton Cemetery. [250]   Starting from Route 30 in Newfane village, take the paved road to the west, passing between the

BRATTLEBORO

Newfane Grange and the Windham County Court House. When the pavement ends, continue along the dirt road that lies straight ahead. The cemetery is on the right-hand side, $5\frac{2}{10}$ miles from Route 30.

It is not generally known that Sir Isaac Newton died and is buried in this quiet corner of southern Vermont. The small cemetery where he is buried is neglected and overgrown. The Newton family plot is in the center, surrounded by an iron railing. Within is a marble obelisk bearing this simple inscription:

SIR ISAAC NEWTON
Died March 24, 1864,
AE. 73.

PATTY
Wife of
SIR ISAAC NEWTON
Died Nov. 27, 1848,
AE. 57.

NORWICH

Old Cemetery. [251] On Mechanic Street, a short distance west of the Norwich Inn.

A small village cemetery, in a pleasant setting on a knoll. Note the large slate marker at the grave of Mrs. Susannah Burton (d. 1775), "Retorned to Dwell with saints on high, where She is Ceased From Every ancious Care & Joind the Geniral Chorus of the Joy." Not far behind this is a ledger stone for the Hon. Jacob Burton (d. 1798), one of the framers of Vermont's Declaration of Independence in January, 1777.

PEACHAM

Oldest Burying Ground. [252] Turn sharply downhill, opposite the village store. The cemetery is ¼ mile ahead, on the right.

Peacham's first graveyard, containing the eighteenth-century stones of the earliest settlers. Cows graze outside the fence, and beyond them is a smaller version of the same beautiful view seen from the big cemetery on the hill. This small cemetery, like the larger one, is immaculately kept.

The gravestone of Deacon Jonathan Elkins and his wife, who came here in 1776, identifies them as the first settlers of Peacham. Notice, nearby, the two "homemade" stones for L. F. and D. F. (d. 1796 and 1800), each decorated with a crude skull-and-crossbones. There is an unusual design on the small stone of Capt. Noah Martin, "A Free and Accepted Mason," (d. 1809).

Peacham Cemetery. [253] Turn sharply uphill beside the village store, past the Congregational Church: the cemetery is at the top of the hill, opposite the old village green.

A very handsome cemetery, carefully maintained, in a beautiful hilltop setting. Tall pine trees stand among the graves; there is an impressive view into the valley to the south. The stones, from the nineteenth century, are for the most part unadorned.

PLYMOUTH

Notch Cemetery. [254] On the other side of Route 100-A from the village of Plymouth: a roadside sign indicates the turn to the cemetery.

A neat set of stone steps guides visitors to the simple graves of Calvin Coolidge (1872–1933) and his wife. The Coolidge marker, in Barre granite, bears the Presidential Seal but no epitaph whatever. Nearby is the Coolidge family plot. The other monuments in Notch Cemetery are of only moderate interest.

The Coolidge home may be visited, a short distance away in the little village of Plymouth. Coolidge, then Vice President, was here on August 3, 1923, when he was notified of the death of President Warren G. Harding. He was sworn in as President by his father, who administered the oath of office with the family bible by the light of a kerosene lamp.

ROCKINGHAM

Rockingham Meeting House Cemetery. [255] The small village of Rockingham lies just to the south of Route 103. A sign by the road indicates the turn to the Old Meeting House. The Meeting House and its cemetery are on a hill above the village road.

The hilltop burying ground beside the Rockingham Meeting House is one of New England's classic cemeteries. There is an austere beauty about the setting: the white frame church building behind, and on the other side a fine view of the farmland in the valley of the Williams River. The stones in the beautifully-kept graveyard date from the 1780's, with some interesting inscriptions. Note for example the marker for Elder Artamus Aldrich "Who was found Dead under his Grist-Mill wheel Feb 9th 1796." At the far back, beside the old grass-covered tomb, is a stone in memory of Miss Eunice Pain (d. 1805 ae. 16) :

> Behold & read a mournfull fate
> Two lovers were sincere
> And one is left without a mate
> The other slumbers here. . . .

The Meeting House itself, an exceptionally handsome building dated 1787, is open to visitors. It retains its original interior: the entire area within is divided into box-like family pews.

ST. ALBANS

Greenwood Cemetery. [256] On Route 7, at the southern edge of town.

The most interesting monument in Greenwood Cemetery is a square marble pillar, south of the driveway, about halfway back from the road in this section. The stone marks the grave of Joseph Partridge Brainerd (1840–64), who graduated from the University of Vermont and enlisted in the Union Army in 1862. The inscription narrates that he "was wounded and taken prisoner by the Rebels in the Wilderness; May 5, 1864 was sent to Andersonville Prison Pen in Georgia where he died on the 11th day of Sept. 1864, entirely and wholly neglected by President Lincoln and murdered with impunity by the Rebels, with thousands of our loyal Soldiers by Starvation, Privation, Exposure, and Abuse."

At the northern edge of the original section is a large obelisk erected to Lawrence Brainerd (1794–1870), a U.S. Senator from Vermont. Brainerd was one of the abolitionist founders of the Republican Party at its Pittsburgh convention of 1856.

SHAFTSBURY CENTER

Old Baptist Churchyard. [257]   On Route 7, next to the Old Baptist Meeting House.

The white marble markers of this beautifully-kept old grave-yard have a perfect setting beside the white church building and against the background of the Green Mountains; in the afternoon of a sunny day the white stones and the white building acquire an almost dazzling brilliance. Among the stones are some superb examples of eighteenth-century work in marble which deserve attention.

Except in certain areas of southern Vermont and western Massachusetts, marble was rarely used for eighteenth-century gravestones. When it came into general use elsewhere, fashions in stonecutting had changed: so that in most places it is un-usual to see, on a white stone, the intricate eighteenth-century designs primarily associated with work in slate. Then again, marble is a relatively soft stone, and old examples of marble markers have often lost their sharpness of detail.

For these reasons the old stones at Shaftsbury are well worth a look. There is a generous number of them, they are brilliantly executed, and they are in remarkably good con-dition. Most of the designs are composed of variations on the same elements: a winged figure of the soul, with floral decora-tions. One interesting exception is the very simple stone, decorated with a heart only, for Mrs. Anne Harris (d. 1799) ; another is the rough "homemade" marble stone for Timothy Puffer (d. 1781). Among the orthodox examples, the finest of all is perhaps that of Lt. Timothy Holcomb, "who died in his return from the Camp, on the 18th of Sept. 1775, in the 36th year of his age." Many of the stones carry epitaphs as well: these are obviously stereotyped, but interesting nevertheless—

MANCHESTER

> You find the place where I am laid,
> To moulder into the Dust,
> As you must be, 'tis only said,
> That I am here the first.

The original church building, on the site of the present one, was the first Baptist church in the State of Vermont.

STOWE

Old Cemetery. [258]   In the center of the village, behind the building holding the town offices and the library.

This small graveyard contains one very curious monument. Near the steps of the entrance is a double headstone of Betsey (d. 1803 ae. 20) and Abigail (d. 1804, ae. 25), both "consort of Capt. Elias Bingham," with a joint epitaph—

> This double call is loud to all
> Let none despise and wonder:
> But to the youth it speaks a truth
> In accents loud as thunder.

There is a marble tablet erected by the town of Stowe in memory of Oliver and Susannah Luce, "the first settlers of the town, haveing moved here April 16, 1794, then an unbroken wilderness." In a far corner is a small monument in cast iron to "Little Douglas, only child of L. E. & C. Payne." There is no date. Such monuments were popular for a brief time in the nineteenth century, and are relatively rare.

VERNON

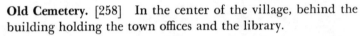

Vernon Cemetery. [259]   On Route 142, north of the village.

This modest cemetery in the unprepossessing town of Vernon is a Golconda of prize epitaphs. Some of them were but poorly

carved and are as a result very difficult to decipher; but the
visitor may assure himself, with a minimum of eyestrain, that
these remarkable verses are not fabrications.

Begin to the left of the gate, among the handsome stones of
the Bridgman family.

> The unfortunate Miranda
> Daughter of John Bridgman
> Whose Remains are here interr'd
> Fell a Prey to the Flames
> That consum'd her father's House
> On the 11th of June 1797
> Aged 28
>
> The rooms below flam'd like a stove
> Anxious for those who slept above
> She ventured on the trembling floor
> It fell, she sank, & rose no more.

(A conscientious epigrapher must report that the left-hand
portion of Miranda's quatrain is now completely missing. It
is here given from earlier transcriptions, never completely
reliable.) Next to Miranda is the following peremptory inscription:

> Pause Mortal!
> and Contemplate the remains
> of Miss Rebecca Cunnable
> the amiable Daughter of
> Samuel Cunnable . . . (d. 1800, ae. 13) . . . .
>
> If Sprightly youth, or human fears,
> Or early piety could save,
> Death had not thus cut short her years.
> But she will Triumph O'er the Grave.

To the right of the gate are the famous gravestones of the Tute family. The grave of Mr. Amos Tute (d. 1790 ae. 60) is marked by a striking white marble stone, with an epitaph which is an amusing morsel of popularized eighteenth-century rationalism. The lines are not original with Mr. Tute. Next to him is buried the truly distinguished member of the family, his wife Jemima. An official marker outside the cemetery testifies to the historical truth of Jemima Tute's exploits; her adventures were described in the novel *Not Without Peril* (1941) by Marguerite Allis.

> Mrs. Jemima Tute
> Successively Relict to Messrs.
> William Phipps, Caleb Howe & Amos Tute.
> The two first were killed by the Indians
> Phipps July 5th AD. 1743
> Howe June 27th 1755.
> When Howe was killed She & her Children
> Then Seven in number
> Were carried into Captivity
> The oldest a Daughter went to France
> And was married to a French Gentleman
> The youngest was torn from her Breast
> And perished with Hunger.
> By the aid of some benevolent Gent'n
> And her own personal Heroism
> She recovered the Rest.
> She had two by her last Husband
> Outlived both him & them
> And died March 7th 1805 aged 82.
> Having past thro more vicissitudes
> And endured more hardships
> Than any of her Contemporaries.
> No more can Savage foes annoy
> Nor aught her widespread Fame Destroy.

Behind Amos and Jemima is something even more remarkable. The whole epitaph is there and can, with difficulty, be read.

> Here lies cut down like unripe Fruit
> A Son of Mr. Amos Tute
> And Mrs. Jemima Tute his Wife
> Call'd Jonathan, of Whose frail Life
> The Days all Summ'd (how Short th'account)
> Scarcely to fourteen years Amount.
> Born on the Twelvth of May was He
> In Seaventeen Hundred Sixty Three
> To Death he fell a helpless Prey
> April the Five & Twentieth Day
> In Sev'nteen Hundred Seventy Seven
> Quitting this World We hope for Heaven.
> But tho his Spirit's fled on High
> His Body mould'ring here must lie.
> Behold th'amazing alteration
> Effected by Inoculation
> The Means improv'd his Life to Save
> Hurried him headlong to the Grave
> Full in the Bloom of Youth he fell
> Alass   What human tongue can tell
> The Mother's Grief, her Anguish Show
> Or paint the Father's heavier Woe:
> Who now no nat'ral offspring has
> His ample Fortune to possess
> To fill his Place, Stand in his Stead
> Or bear his Name, When he is dead.
> So God Ordain'd, His Ways are Just
> Tho Empires Crumble in to Dust
> Life and the World Mere Bubbles are
> Set loose to these, for Heaven prepare.

W A L L I N G F O R D

Green Hill Cemetery. [260]   On Route 7, at the southern edge of village.

An attractive cemetery, stretching in terraced levels quite some distance up a hillside. The majority of the stones are nineteenth century and later; in the older section near the road, however, there are some stones of particular interest. These include a few examples of late eighteenth-century stonecutting in marble (e.g., the interesting stone of Mr. Abraham Jackson, d. 1791); a pair of large stones, side by side, marking the graves of Kent Ives and his relict Mary, on which the reliefs show each of the couple grieving for the other; and the stone nearby of Mr. Alvin White, bearing a finger pointing straight to heaven and the misspelled legend, "Past On."

The most engaging stone in this cemetery is toward the north side and not far from the road. The inscription begins, "Fell a victim to Death's cold hands on the 22nd of July 1812, Mr. Norman Towner / Ag'd 27 / one of societie's brightest ornaments. . . ."

W E S T M I N S T E R

Westminster Cemetery. [261]   On Route 5, at the northern edge of the village.

This very attractive cemetery contains an interesting reminder of the confused and troubled history of this part of New England before it became the independent State of Vermont. The cause of the trouble was the failure of the British Crown to define an eastern boundary for the State of New York. Much of what is now Vermont was settled under grants of land issued by Governor Wentworth of New Hampshire, beginning in 1749. New York subsequently claimed the same area, reaching east to the Connecticut River. This claim

232

MONTPELIER

was officially upheld in 1764, and New York State began issuing its own patents covering the Vermont land. The settlers holding land under the earlier New Hampshire Grants, naturally enough, refused to move; they began a campaign of resistance to the authority of the Yorkers. On March 13, 1775 two Westminster men were killed in a violent incident at the nearby Cumberland County Court House, as local patriots tried to prevent the York State magistrates from holding session. Shortly thereafter, the outbreak of the Revolutionary War made the British the common enemy of all parties to the land dispute. A meeting at Westminster in January, 1777 declared the independence of the State of Vermont. The continued hostility of New York State kept the Continental Congress from including Vermont among the original thirteen states, and it was not until 1791, after an indemnification of $30,000 had been paid to New York, that Vermont was finally admitted to the Union.

In the cemetery is a monument erected by the State of Vermont to William French and Daniel Houghton, the two men killed in the Westminster "Massacre" of 1775. Next to it stands a recent copy in slate of the original gravestone of William French, "who Was Shot at Westminster, March the 13th, 1775, by the hands of Cruel Ministereal tools of Georg the 3d.; in the Corthouse, at a 11 a Clock at Night; in the 22d year of his Age."

> Here William French his Body lies.
> For Murder his Blood for Vengeance cries.
> King Georg the third his Tory crew
> tha with a Bawl his head Shot threw.
> For Liberty and his Countrys Good.
> he Lost his Life his Dearest blood.

Besides this gem, the cemetery contains a fine assortment of stones. Notice, for instance, the intriguing portrait face on the marker of Mrs. Mary Wright, d. 1798 ae. 27.

WILLISTON

Old Williston Graveyard. [262]   On Route 2 at the eastern edge of the village. (There is a second cemetery ½ mile further east.)

Standing by itself at the western end of the cemetery is a huge monument in Barre granite to Thomas Chittenden (1730–97), the first Governor of Vermont, who made his home in Williston. One side of the base of the monument shows a portrait head of Chittenden; the other side, the Ship of State riding a stormy sea. Near the center of the cemetery proper is the Governor's original gravestone. It makes an interesting contrast to the monument erected by the State a hundred years later.

Note also, among the older graves, the fine portrait stone of Mr. Samuel Smith (d. 1800) .

Additional Notes

ᘒ GRAVESTONE RUBBING ᘒ

One reason for the increased interest in New England cemeteries is the growing popularity in this country of gravestone
rubbing. This is simply the process of producing on a sheet of
paper a copy of the engraving on a stone by rubbing a piece
of colored wax over the paper, which is held against the surface
of the stone. Brass rubbing has long been popular in England,
where tombs are sometimes covered by engraved brass portraits
of the deceased. There are no funeral brasses in New England,
but the images obtained from the best slate stones are equally
interesting. Those who already enjoy gravestone rubbing need
no instruction from this book. Those who would like to try it
are informed that the necessary materials (special paper and
special wax) may be readily obtained from a growing number
of artist's supply stores—particularly in New England, where
the best stones for rubbing are to be found. All that is really
required in the way of technique is patience: presumably each
rubber possesses the degree of perfectionism he demands in the
finished product. It might be added as a word of caution that
it is a good idea to get permission before rubbing any stones,
if there is anyone around who might reasonably be asked.
Gravestones have been damaged by careless people on occasion,

and in some places—most notably the city of Boston—all gravestone rubbing is expressly prohibited.

⌒ GENEALOGY ⌒

Many visitors to New England are interested, to some degree at
least, in amateur genealogy. Even if one knows the precise
town where an ancestor lived and died, it is a good idea to try
to narrow the possibilities before going out to look for his
grave. The best resource of all is a list of burials in the cemeteries of a town. Where these include older graves, they have
generally been compiled in later years by a local historical
society: so the first step is to write to the local historical society,
if there is one, to find out whether they have any such information. To determine whether there is in fact such a society,
refer to the *Directory of Historical Societies and Agencies in
the United States and Canada,* found in any good library; it is
published by the American Association for State and Local
History in Nashville, Tennessee. If a town has no local historical society, the next place to try is the town clerk's office. A
town clerk should be able to provide a list of all the cemeteries
in town, including the old and abandoned ones. This is vital
information, as some towns in New England have literally
scores of small, forgotten cemeteries scattered in the areas of
earlier settlement.

⌒ FINDING CEMETERIES ⌒

Along with each description of a cemetery in this book are
what should be foolproof directions for getting there. But finding a small, out-of-the-way cemetery for genealogical or other

purposes can be a difficult and time-consuming process. The best places to begin asking directions are a historical society, the town clerk's office, or the public library: even if the people in these places do not have the information, they may know someone who does. Once started, there is nothing to do but to keep asking. A good description of the procedure is provided in this account by Mr. Chester Trout, a New England cemetery fancier who lives in East Lansing, Michigan:

We have learned that most every old town has a cemetery somewhere. It is good to seek out someone in the community who is familiar with its history, and make inquiry about the "old" cemetery. We most always get a response, or at least referral to someone else better able to serve us. This has caused us to meet some interesting people. Often times, we doubt if their directions are correct after driving for what seems like hours over narrow roads and even cowpaths; but usually, if we follow their advice, we are well rewarded. I am reminded of an experience in Grafton, Vermont, when late one afternoon we started what turned out to be a four-day search for the Rebecca Parks stone. We were anxious to get a rubbing of this stone for our collection and it seemed no monumental task to find it in such a small town as Grafton. We started our search at the Post Office, as we often do. They directed us to a road one mile north of town. We drove up and down that country road for some time and were about to return to the Post Office and tell them they were all wet, that there wasn't any such road out there at a right angle to the county road; but just then an old car with three men in it came swerving round the corner. They were forced to stop because they almost collided with us. This gave us an opportunity to ask them if there was an old cemetery in the vicinity. These fellows were enjoying their after-work beer and were quite happy, so we had little confidence in the directions they gave us, especially since it was the same as we were given in town. I told them we had driven that road over and again, but they swore that if we would go back to within a mile of town and turn left we would find our burying ground. We pursued our course in a more systematic way, inspecting every gap in the fence row as we went. Finally, we saw a small opening. I swung the car across the ditch and down a cowpath through the holler. It seemed like a stupid thing to do, but I proceeded with caution on up the other side of the hill and just as we crested, we were very richly rewarded. On our immediate right across a stone fence and through a wooden gate swung in stone posts, was a sight to behold. Nestled there in a five-acre clearing among the hardwoods that were at the very peak of fall colors was a resting place for approximately two hundred souls that had been entombed for as long as two hundred years. The sun was just about to set and along with the brilliance of the trees was the play of reds and golds upon the marble grave markers. We did some rubbing here; however, the Parks stone was not here. Well, we spent the next four days following this same pattern of activity, during which time we met many more interesting persons like the old gentleman sitting out back of his house in his old rocking chair swatting flies and singing "Rock of Ages". . . . We did finally make inquiry of the county clerk and were guided to the Rebecca Parks stone.

Acknowledgments

The author wishes to express his appreciation to the following for their valuable assistance:

CONNECTICUT   Morris W. Abbott, Milford; Mrs. George B. Armstead, Jr., Historical Society of Glastonbury; Frances H. Benjamin, Goshen Historical Society; Robert J. Blair, Chester; Mrs. Edward Breed, Mystic; Catherine C. Calhoun, Torrington Historical Society; Mrs. Alfred Cramer, Noank Historical Society; Elmer Garrett, Bridgewater Historical Society; Thompson R. Harlow, Connecticut Historical Society, Hartford; Joel E. Helander, Guilford Keeping Society; Earl W. Hoffman, Broad Brook; Mrs. Robert Hummel, Plainville Historical Society; Mrs. Asa W. Hyde, Colchester; Elizabeth B. Knox, New London County Historical Society; Robert R. Macdonald, New Haven Colony Historical Society; Nellie E. McKnight, Ellington; Francis P. Mellen, Easton Historical Society; Mrs. G. R. Merwin, Wilton Historical Society; Esther K. Neff, Higganum; George R. Perry, Bristol Historical Society; George O. Pratt, Fairfield Historical Society; Dorothy T. Schling, Danbury Historical Society; W. S. Tower, Jr., Essex Historical Society; Campbell Wilson, Windsor Historical Society; Mary Wright, Haddam Historical Association.

MAINE   Marjorie Camp, Bar Harbor Historical Society; Richard L. Castner, Waldoboro; Mrs. Adelaide Day, Kennebunkport; Col. Thurlow R. Dunning, Freeport; Maxine Forster, Saco; Stephen C. Foster, Brunswick; George W. Garniss, Yarmouth His-

Acknowledgments

torical Society; Jonathan D. McKallip, Orono; Donna T. Orwin, Machias; Miss L. M. Prince, Bangor Historical Society; Richard Shaw, Bangor.

MASSACHUSETTS   Mrs. William S. Annin, Richmond; The Boston Athenaeum; Col. Oliver B. Brown, Falmouth Historical Society; Mrs. Charles S. Connington, Barre Historical Society; Danvers Historical Society; Harold J. Davis, Chelmsford Historical Society; Essex Institute, Salem; Mrs. Walter Flinn, North Andover Historical Society; Daniel Farber, Worcester; Mary B. Gifford, Fall River Historical Society; Harriet Reisen Gold, Cambridge; Mrs. James Gosling, Marblehead; Stanley Greenberg, Northampton; David L. Gunner, Wellesley Historical Society; Mrs. Donald F. Haines, Petersham; Ruth Hill, Beverly Historical Society; John Kittredge, Worcester; Wallace Kneeland, Topsfield; Karl and Marianne Lipsky, New Marlboro; Mrs. Charles M. Litchfield, Buckland Historical Society; Wolfgang Lowy, Sturbridge Historical Commission; Mrs. A. E. Lumley, Pelham Historical Commission; Mrs. J. D. MacFarland, Northborough Historical Society; Donald McClure, Barnstable; Avon Neal, North Brookfield; Eileen Nuttall, Cheshire Historical Commission; Duncan B. Oliver, South Easton; Lester W. Parker, Brimfield; Margaret S. Parker, North Reading; George Adams Parkhurst, Chelmsford Historical Commission; Judy C. Peters, Lenox; Muriel N. Peters, Dedham Historical Society; Mrs. Harold C. Pierce, Jr., Stockbridge; Lillian E. Preiss, Sheffield Historical Society; Helen Raymond, Hull Historical Society; Winifred D. Sayer, Amherst; Mrs. Doheny H. Sessions, Hadley; Donald S. Smith, Berkshire County Historical Society; George W. Stetson, Middleboro; Frances P. Tapley, Sterling Historical Society; Dorothy W. Taylor, Shelburne Falls; Juliette Tomlinson, Connecticut Valley Historical Museum, Springfield; Harold G. Travis, Weston Historical Society; Mrs. Robert S. Trim, Annawan Historical Society; Leroy H. True, Nantucket Historical Association; Nina R. Tryon, Monterey; Harold S. Walker, Lynn Historical Society; Dorothy Wentworth, Duxbury; Donnell B. Young, Hanover.

NEW HAMPSHIRE   Mr. and Mrs. Homer J. Belletete, Jaffrey; Kenneth C. Cramer, Dartmouth College Archives; Mrs. Goodhue Crocker, Canaan; Elizabeth C. Greenie, Peterborough Historical Society; Arnold J. Grover, Portsmouth Historical Society; Constance G. Hobbs, South Effingham; Mrs. David D. Merrill, Exeter Historical Society; Katharine S. Morrill, New Hampshire Historical Society, Concord; Helen E. Nute, North Conway; Virginia G. Plisko, Manchester Historic Association; David R. Proper, Keene; Dorothy W. Sears, Lyme; Elizabeth C. Spring, Nashua Historical Society; Howard E. Turner, Salem; Philip A. Wilcox, Durham Historic Association; Mrs. Clair E. Wyman, West Swanzey.

RHODE ISLAND   Alice B. Almy, Bristol Historical & Preservation Society; J. P. Black, Providence; Carlton C. Brownell, Little Compton Historical Society; Edwin W. Connelly, Newport; Mrs. Pickett M. Greig, Jamestown; Mrs. Leonard Panaggio, Preservation Society of Newport County; Marjorie W. Schunke, Wakefield; Miss G. Steadman, Block Island Historical Society.

VERMONT   Charles G. Bennett, Bennington; Donald M. Boyer, Riverton; Philip T. Copeland, Highgate Center; Janet C. Greene, West Dover; Walter Hard, Jr., Burlington; Helen B. Hartman, Manchester Center; Robin Kaemmerlen, West Dover; Charlotte Peck, Wilmington; Alfred F. Rosa, Burlington.

Index of Persons

Adams, John, 130. *See also* Tucker, Commander Samuel
Adams, John Quincy
  grave, 130
  in *Amistad* case, 19
Adams, Samuel, 85
Agassiz, Louis, 91
Alcott family, 94
Alden, Jonathan, 100
Alden, Priscilla, 102
Aldrich, Thomas B., 91
Allen, Ethan, 212
Allen, General Ira, 212–3
Allen, Reverend Thomas (d. 1810), 128
Allen, Thomas (d. 1882), 128

Barnum, Phineas T., 7
Beecher, Lyman, 32
Belmont, August, 196
Berkeley, George. *See* Johnson, Samuel
Billings, Josh. *See* Shaw, Henry Wheeler
Blount, F. Nelson, 159
Borden, Lizzie, 103

Bradford, William, 129
Bradstreet, Anne, 133
Brady, Al, 52
Brainerd, Lawrence, 225
Brown, Nicholas, 198
Browning, Robert. *See* Thaxter, Celia
Buck, Colonel Jonathan, 55
Bulfinch, Thomas, 91
Bull, Ephraim, 94
Bull, John (stonecarving by), 193
Buttrick, Colonel John, 93

Camden, Lord (Charles Pratt) (invoked in epitaph), 90
Cather, Willa, 165
Channing, William Ellery, 91
Chittenden, Thomas, 235
Church, Benjamin, 192
Churchill, Winston S. (ancestors), 8
Cinque, Joseph (*Amistad* prisoner), 19

Coolidge, Calvin
  ancestors, 144
  grave, 224
Cummings, E. E., 84
Cutter, Carrie, 170

Dexter, Lord Timothy, 120–1
Dickinson, Emily, 78
Dix, Dorothy, 91
Dorr, Thomas W.
  "Anti-Governor" of R.I., 188
  grave, 199
Drake, Joseph Rodman. *See* Halleck, Fitz-Greene
Drew, Daniel. *See* Fisk, James
Dwight, Timothy, 32

Eddy, Mary Baker, 90
Edwards, Jonathan, xi–xii
Eldred, John, 191
Emerson, Ralph Waldo, 94

Faneuil, Peter, 85
Fenwick, Lady Alice, 36

Index of Persons

Fisk, James, 210–2
Franklin, Benjamin (ancestors), 85
French, Daniel Chester
 cemetery sculpture by, 85
 grave, 94
Frost, Robert, 208

Garfield, James A. (ancestors), 144
Garrison, William Lloyd, 84
Gibson, Charles Dana, 91
Gilman, Nicholas, 160
Goddard, Robert H., 150
Goodyear, Charles, 32
Gould, Jay. See Fisk, James
Gray, Captain S. L., 26

Hale, Edward Everett, x, 84
Hale, Nathan, 9–10
Hall, Lyman, 40
Halleck, Fitz-Greene, xi, 22–3
Hamlin, Hannibal, 51
Hancock, John
 ancestors, 16, 130
 grave, 85
Harrison, Benjamin (ancestors), 147
Harvard, John, 87
Hawthorne, Nathaniel, 94
Hinman, Clark T., 220
Hoar, Leonard, 130
Holland, Josiah G., 138

Holmes, Oliver Wendell
 grave, 91
 poem dedicating cemetery, 127
Hooker, Thomas (settles Hartford, Conn.), 24
Howe, Julia Ward, 91
Huntington family, 33–4
Huntington, Samuel, 34

Igloo, 99
Inot, Robert, 118
Ives, Charles, 11

Johnson, Samuel, 38–9
Johnson, William Samuel, 39

Kellogg, Elijah, 56

Langdon, John, 175
Law, Jonathan, 28
Lincoln, Abraham (attacked in epitaph), 225
Longfellow, Henry Wadsworth
 grave, 91
 poem on *Enterprise-Boxer* sea fight, 63
 poem on Jewish Cemetery, Newport, R.I., 197
Lovecraft, H. P., 199
Lowell, Amy, 91

Macdonough, Commodore Thomas, 28
McKay, Gordon, 128

Mather, Cotton, 84
Mather, Increase, 84

Newton, Sir Isaac (Newfane, Vt., namesake), 222
Norton, Charles Eliot, 91
Nurse, Rebecca, 96

O'Neill, Eugene, 84
Otis, James, 85
 epitaph composed by, 145

Paine, Robert Treat, 85
Palmer, Joseph, 110–1; *ill.*, 101
Parkman, Francis, 91
Parris, Elizabeth, 97
Paterson, General John, 110
Peavey, James, 52
Percival, Captain John ("Mad Jack"), 145
Perry, Commodore Matthew Calbraith, 194, 196
Perry, Commodore Oliver Hazard, 194, 196
Phillips, Wendell, 118
Pierce, Franklin
 ancestors, 147
 grave, 158
Preble, Commodore Edward, 62

Quincy, Josiah, 91

Revere, Paul, 85

Roosevelt, Franklin D. (ancestors), 147
Root, George Frederick, 124

Saint-Gaudens, Augustus (cemetery sculpture by), 138, 196
Savage, Samuel Phillips, 146
Sedgwick, Catharine Maria (epitaph composed by), 140
Sewall, Samuel (d. 1730).
  diary quoted, 99. See also Parris, Elizabeth
Sewall, Samuel (d. 1814), 68
Shaw, Henry Wheeler ("Josh Billings"), 109
Smith, Joseph (ancestors), 142
Standish, Miles, 100
Stark, Elizabeth ("Molly"), 168

Stark, General John, 168
Stevens, John (stonecarving by), 193
Stratton, Charles S. ("General Tom Thumb"), 7
Stuart, Gilbert, 82
Sumner, Charles, 91

Tenney, Mrs. Tabitha, 160
Thaxter, Celia, 57
Thomas, Robert B., 146
Thomas, Theodore, 91
Thoreau, Henry David, 94
Thumb, General Tom. See Stratton, Charles S.
Tichenor, Isaac, 208
Tituba. See Parris, Elizabeth
Treat, Robert, 28
Trumbull family, xii, 26
Tucker, Commander Samuel, 60–1

Uncas (Mohegan Indian sachem), 32

Vanderbilt, Cornelius. See Fisk, James

Webster, Daniel, 115–6
Webster, Noah, 32
Wheelock, Eleazar, 162
Whipple, William, 175
Whitney, Eli, xiii, 32
Whittier, John Greenleaf
  epitaph composed by, 96
  grave, 78
  poem on *Palatine* incident, 185
  poem quoted in epitaph, 51
Williams, Abigail. See Parris, Elizabeth
Williams, William, 26
Winslow, Josiah, 116
Winthrop, John, 86
Wooster, Brigadier David, 10
Worcester, Jonathan (stonecarving by), 105–6

General Index

Abolitionism, 18–20, 28, 91, 118, 225
Accidental death, 20, 64, 88, 104, 120, 126–7, 134, 141, 164, 169, 197
Adam and Eve, depicted on gravestone, 187
African inscription, 220
African scene, depicted on gravestone, 220
Amistad incident, 18–20
Amputated leg, gravestone for, 168
Andersonville prison, 61, 225
Angel, 112, 114, 122, 134, 175, 196, 207, 208, 213, 218, *ill.*, 182, 195, 227
Animal cemetery, 99
Apparition on gravestone, 53–4, 55
Arboretum, 90, 198
Artists, 82, 85, 91, 94, 138, 196
Atheism, 65, 214

Authors, 22–3, 32, 51, 56, 57, 63, 78, 84, 91, 94, 96, 109, 118, 127, 133, 138, 140, 146, 160, 165, 185, 197, 199, 208

Baptist Church, 64, 170
Barbary pirates, 62
Barre, Mass., *ill.*, 83
Barre, Vt., *ill.*, 209
Bat, depicted on gravestone, 114
Battle
  Bennington, 128, 168, 208
  Concord Bridge, 79, 93
  Lake Champlain, 28
  Lake Erie, 196
  Lexington, 79, 111–2
  The *Margaretta*, 58–60
Bed, depicted on gravestone, 207
Bennington (Vt.), Battle of, 128, 168, 208
Body-in-coffin motif, xv, 27, 135

Boston, Mass., *ill.*, 89
Boston Massacre, 85
Boston Tea Party, 146, 150
Brattleboro, Vt., *ill.*, 221
Brewster, Mass., *ill.*, 95
Bridgeport, Conn., *ill.*, 15
Brown University, 198
Businessmen, 85, 128, 198, 210–2

Candle-snuffer monument, 104
Carving styles, evolution of, xv
Cask burial, 26
Cast iron monument, 228
Charter Oak, 12
Cherub
  "idealized," xv
  "individualized," xv, 115, 126, 146
Christ, life of, depicted on gravestone, 165
Church, building moved, 191–2
Civil War
  missing soldier, 67

Civil War *(cont.)*
naval engagement, 26
N.H. soldiers killed, 168
nurse, 170
unknown Confederate soldier, 55
See also Andersonville prison
Civil War memorial, 51
Clergymen, 24, 32, 38–9, 84, 90, 91, 97, 99, 128, 162, 220
Clock motif, xvi
Coffin, depicted on gravestone, 164
Columbia University, 38
Composers, 11, 91, 124
Concord grape, 94
Concord (Mass.), Battle of, 79, 93
Congress, U.S., 39, 212, 234
Connecticut River settlements, 24
Constitution, U.S., signer, 160
Constitution, U.S.S., 62, 145
Courtship of Miles Standish, The, 102
Cuttingsville, Vt., *ill.*, 215

Dartmouth College, 162
Death (allegorical figure), 86
Death at sea, 37, 57, 62, 67, 69, 118, 130,

134, 190. *See also* Shipwreck
Declaration of Independence, signer, 26, 34, 40, 175
Deerfield Massacre, 100
Dog, depicted on gravestone, 44, 91, 99
"Dorr War," 188–90
Dragon, depicted on gravestone, 41
Duxbury, Mass., *ill.*, 76

Egyptian gateway, 17, 32, 90
Enterprise-Boxer engagement. *See* War of 1812
European cemeteries, 85, 99

Face, depicted on gravestone. *See* Stylized face motif
Fairfield, Conn., *ill.*, 5
Fertility symbol, xvi, 80, 87, 147
Filigree decoration, 126
Flower motif, xvi
"Foster's Rubicon," 60
Freemason, 55, 127, 160, 223
French and Indian War, sea battle, 138
Fruitlands community, 111
Funeral brass, 237

"Garden cemetery," 84, 90
Geometric decoration, 105, 115, 126
Georgia, 40
God, represented on gravestone, 194
Grafton, Vt., 239–40
Granite gravestone, eighteenth century, 127

Harvard College, 87, 123, 133
Heart motif, xvi, 88
Hebrew inscription. *See* Jewish cemetery
Historical society, 238
Homemade gravestone, 16, 71, 105, 156, 223, 226
Hourglass motif, xvi, 114, 174; *ill.*, 173
House gravestone, 136; *ill.*, 143
Huguenot, 85

Indian burying place, 17, 31, 41, 108, 121, 187
Indian captive, 100, 230–1
Indian raid, 171
Indians, 17, 31, 138, 187
Inventors, 32, 150
Invisible cemetery, 149–50

Jaffrey, N.H., *ill.*, 161
Japan, 196

Jewish cemetery, 13, 196–7

King Philip's War, 30, 34, 192
Knickerbocker Wits, 22

Lake Champlain, Battle of, 28
Lake Erie, Battle of, 196
Latin inscription, 56, 145, 164
Ledger Stone, 197, 222
Leominster, Mass., *ill.*, 101
Lexington (Mass.), Battle of, 79, 111–2
Lexington, Mass., *ill.*, 107
Lighthouse, depicted on gravestone, 16
Lion, sculpture, *ill.*, 113
Locomotive, depicted on gravestone, 10, 128, 159. *See also* Train wreck
Lowell, Mass., *ill.*, 113

Manchester, Vt., *ill.*, 227
Marble gravestone, eighteenth century, 109, 206, 226, 232
Margaretta, The, Battle of, 58–60
Marlborough, Mass., *ill.*, 119
Marlborough, N.H., *ill.*, 154

Mausoleum, 112, 128, 213
Mayflower passenger, 130
Millstone as grave marker, 12
Missionary, 138–9, 220
Modern sculpture, 51, 85
Mohegan Indians, 31
Montpelier, Vt., *ill.*, 233
Mormonism, 142
Mortality symbol, xvi
"Mother Goose," 86
Multiple grave, 98–9, 135
Multiple headstone, 25, 26, 38, 105, 157, 193, 218, 228
Murder, 102–3, 106
Murder victim, 124, 171, 207

Narragansett Indians, 31, 187
Newburyport, Mass., *ill.*, 125, 131, 137
"New Hampshire Grants," 177–8, 232–4
Newport, R.I., *ill.*, 182, 189
Northwestern University, 220

Old Farmers' Almanac, The, x, 146
"Old Ironsides." *See Constitution, U.S.S.*
One-Gun Battery, 191

Palatine incident, 184–6
Palatine light, 186
Peacham, Vt., *ill.*, ii, 204
Peterborough, N.H., *ill.*, 173
Photograph on gravestone, 62, 99
Pietá, 219
Pointing-finger motif, 81, 232; *ill.*, 167
Portrait stone, vx, 22, 26, 40, 44, 71, 80, 87, 88, 108, 114, 117, 120, 121, 129, 144, 158, 160, 166, 177, 184, 234, 235; *ill.*, 119, 131
Presidents, U.S., 19, 60–1, 130, 144, 147, 158, 224, 225
Putnam, Conn., *ill.*, 29

Quakerism, 191

Republican Party, 225
Revolutionary War
Battle of Bennington, 128, 168, 208
Battle of Concord Bridge, 79, 93
Battle of Lexington, 79, 111
Battle of The *Margaretta,* 58–60
espionage in, 9–10
French allies, 33, 41, 86
Mass. Board of War, 146
One-Gun Battery, 191

Revolutionary War
(*cont.*)
privateer, 60
Quebec campaign,
10
soldiers quartered in
Stratford, Conn.,
10
Tories, 40
Tory Raids, 10
Rhode Island constitu-
tional reform cri-
sis, 188–90
Rockingham, Vt., *ill.,*
217
Russian cemetery, 64

Sailing ship, depicted
on gravestone, 16,
27, 52, 62, 79, 86,
235
Salem Village (Mass.) ,
96–8
Savannah, The, 118
Saybrook Fort
(Conn.) , 36
Seventh-Day Adven-
tist Church, 168
Sheaf motif, 112; *ill.,*
233
Ship, depicted on
gravestone. *See*
Sailing ship, de-
picted on grave-
stone
Shipwreck, 58, 121. *See
also Palatine* in-
cident
Signature, on grave-
stone, 219
Skeleton motif, xv,
114, 133

Skull-and-crossbones
motif, xv, 106, 114,
123, 223
Skull motif, 147; *ill.,*
125
Slave, 18–20, 90, 93,
139, 165, 194
Slave Monument, 90
Smallpox, 30
Snake, depicted on
gravestone, 114,
187
Soldiers, 9, 10, 26, 28,
55, 60–1, 62, 93,
110, 145, 168, 191,
192, 194, 196, 212
Soul, represented on
gravestone, 139,
171. *See also* Soul-
and-wings motif
Soul-and-wings motif,
xv, 10, 43, 109,
121, 166, 226; *ill.,*
95, 119, 137, 189
South Windham, Me.,
ill., 48
Sphinx monument, 90
Springfield, Mass., *ill.,*
143
Statesmen, 8, 16, 26, 28,
34, 39, 40, 51, 68,
85, 86, 91, 115–6,
129, 130, 145, 146,
160, 175, 208, 212–
3, 225, 235
Sterling, Mass., *ill.,* 149
Stockbridge Indians,
138
Stonecarvers, 105–6,
193
Stonecarving, styles,
xv–xvi

Stylized face motif, 17,
27, 42, 105, 206
Sun motif, 213
Sun-and-moon motif,
69, 114, 160
Sunburst motif, xvi, 8,
114, 139
Sundial, 12
Sunflower motif, xvi,
25, 135

Table stone, 25, 41–2,
79, 105, 109, 147,
156, 159, 163, 192
Ticonderoga, Fort,
(N.Y.) , 8, 212
Time (allegorical fig-
ure) , 86, 133
Train wreck, 128, 132
Tree-stump motif, 6,
112, 220
Tripolitan War, 62,
145
Tunxis Indians, 17

Urn-and-willow motif,
xvi, 176; *ill.,* 83

Vegetable symbol, xvi,
80, 87
Vermont statehood,
212, 234
Vermont, University
of, 212
"Vinegar Bible," 176
Vine motif, xvi, 27, 50,
88

War of 1812, 37
Battle of Lake
Champlain, 28
Battle of Lake Erie,
196

War of 1812 *(cont.)*
  Enterprise-Boxer
    engagement, 63
  U.S.S. *Constitution*
    in, 145

Washington, N.H., *ill.*,
  167
Westerly, R.I., *ill.*, 195
Westminster Massacre,
  232–4

William Henry, Fort,
  (Me.) , 61
Witch, 55, 71, 96–8
Yale College, 36
York, Me., *ill.*, 59